HMH SCIENCE DIMENSIONS™
CELLS AND HEREDITY

Module B

This Write-In Book belongs to

_____

Teacher/Room

_____

Houghton Mifflin Harcourt™

Consulting Authors

Michael A. DiSpezio

Global Educator
North Falmouth,
Massachusetts

Michael DiSpezio
has authored many
HMH instructional
programs for Science
and Mathematics.
He has also authored
numerous trade books and multimedia
programs on various topics and hosted dozens
of studio and location broadcasts for various
organizations in the U.S. and worldwide. Most
recently, he has been working with educators
to provide strategies for implementing the Next
Generation Science Standards, particularly
the science and engineering practices,
cross-cutting concepts, and the use of Evidence
Notebooks. To all his projects, he brings his
extensive background in science, his expertise
in classroom teaching at the elementary,
middle, and high school levels, and his deep
experience in producing interactive and
engaging instructional materials.

Marjorie Frank

*Science Writer and Content-
Area Reading Specialist*
Brooklyn, New York

An educator and linguist
by training, a writer
and poet by nature,
Marjorie Frank has
authored and designed
a generation of
instructional materials in all subject areas,
including past HMH Science programs. Her
other credits include authoring science issues of
an award-winning children's magazine, writing
game-based digital assessments, developing
blended learning materials for young children,
and serving as instructional designer and
co-author of pioneering school-to-work
software. In addition, she has served on the
adjunct faculty of Hunter, Manhattan, and
Brooklyn Colleges, teaching courses in science
methods, literacy, and writing. For *HMH Science
Dimensions™*, she has guided the development
of our K–2 strands and our approach to making
connections between NGSS and Common Core
ELA/literacy standards.

Acknowledgments

Cover credits: (lily cross-section) ©Houghton Mifflin Harcourt; (lily anther cross-section) ©Garry DeLong/Oxford Scientific/
Getty Images.

Section Header Master Art: (human cells, illustration) ©Sebastian Kaulitzki/Science Photo Library/Corbis

Copyright © 2018 by Houghton Mifflin Harcourt Publishing Company

Printed in the U.S.A.

ISBN   978-0-544-86095-7

4 5 6 7 8 9 10   0877   25 24 23 22 21 20 19 18 17

4500645471   A B C D E F G

Michael R. Heithaus, Ph.D.

Dean, College Of Arts, Sciences & Education Professor, Department Of Biological Sciences
Florida International University
Miami, Florida

Mike Heithaus joined the FIU Biology Department in 2003, has served as Director of the Marine Sciences Program and Executive Director of the School of Environment, Arts, and Society, which brings together the natural and social sciences and humanities to develop solutions to today's environmental challenges. He now serves as Dean of the College of Arts, Sciences & Education. His research focuses on predator-prey interactions and the ecological importance of large marine species. He has helped to guide the development of Life Science content in *HMH Science Dimensions™*, with a focus on strategies for teaching challenging content as well as the science and engineering practices of analyzing data and using computational thinking.

Cary I. Sneider, Ph.D.

Associate Research Professor
Portland State University
Portland, Oregon

While studying astrophysics at Harvard, Cary Sneider volunteered to teach in an Upward Bound program and discovered his real calling as a science teacher. After teaching middle and high school science in Maine, California, Costa Rica and Micronesia, he settled for nearly three decades at Lawrence Hall of Science in Berkeley, California, where he developed skills in curriculum development and teacher education. Over his career Cary directed more than 20 federal, state, and foundation grant projects, and was a writing team leader for the Next Generation Science Standards. He has been instrumental in ensuring *HMH Science Dimensions™* meets the high expectations of the NGSS and provides an effective three-dimensional learning experience for all students.

Program Advisors

Paul D. Asimow
Eleanor and John R. McMillan Professor of Geology and Geochemistry
California Institute of Technology
Pasadena, California

Dr. Eileen Cashman
Professor
Humboldt State University
Arcata, California

Elizabeth A. De Stasio
Raymond J. Herzog Professor of Science
Lawrence University
Appleton, Wisconsin

Perry Donham
Lecturer
Boston University
Boston, Massachusetts

Shila Garg, Ph.D.
Emerita Professor of Physics
Former Dean of Faculty & Provost
The College of Wooster
Wooster, Ohio

Tatiana A. Krivosheev
Professor of Physics
Clayton State University
Morrow, Georgia

Mark B. Moldwin
Professor of Space Sciences and Engineering
University of Michigan
Ann Arbor, Michigan

Kelly Y. Neiles, Ph.D.
Assistant Professor of Chemistry
St. Mary's College of Maryland
St. Mary's City, Maryland

Dr. Sten Odenwald
Astronomer
NASA Goddard Spaceflight Center
Greenbelt, Maryland

Bruce W. Schafer
Executive Director
Oregon Robotics Tournament & Outreach Program
Beaverton, Oregon

Barry A. Van Deman
President and CEO
Museum of Life and Science
Durham, North Carolina

Kim Withers, Ph.D.
Assistant Professor
Texas A&M University-Corpus Christi
Corpus Christi, Texas

Adam D. Woods, Ph.D.
Professor
California State University, Fullerton
Fullerton, California

Classroom Reviewers

Cynthia Book, Ph.D.
John Barrett Middle School
Carmichael, California

Katherine Carter, M.Ed.
Fremont Unified School District
Fremont, California

Theresa Hollenbeck, M.Ed.
Winston Churchill Middle School
Carmichael, California

Kathryn S. King
Science and AVID Teacher
Norwood Jr. High School
Sacramento, California

Donna Lee
Science/STEM Teacher
Junction Ave. K8
Livermore, California

Rebecca S. Lewis
Science Teacher
North Rockford Middle School
Rockford, Michigan

Bryce McCourt
8th Grade Science Teacher/Middle School Curriculum Chair
Cudahy Middle School
Cudahy, Wisconsin

Sarah Mrozinski
Teacher
St. Sebastian School
Milwaukee, Wisconsin

Raymond Pietersen
Science Program Specialist
Elk Grove Unified School District
Elk Grove, California

Richard M. Stec, M.A. – Curriculum, Instruction, and Supervision
District Science Supervisor
West Windsor-Plainsboro
Regional School District
West Windsor, New Jersey

Anne Vitale
STEM Supervisor
Randolph Middle School
Randolph, New Jersey

You are a scientist!
You are naturally curious.

Have you ever wondered . . .

- why is it difficult to catch a fly?
- how a new island can appear in an ocean?
- how to design a great tree house?
- how a spacecraft can send messages across the solar system?

HMH SCIENCE **DIMENSIONS**™

will *SPARK* your curiosity!

AND prepare you for

✓	tomorrow
✓	next year
✓	college or career
✓	life!

Where do you see yourself in 15 years?

Observe

Collect Data

Be a scientist.
Work like real scientists work.

Analyze

Be an engineer.
Solve problems like engineers do.

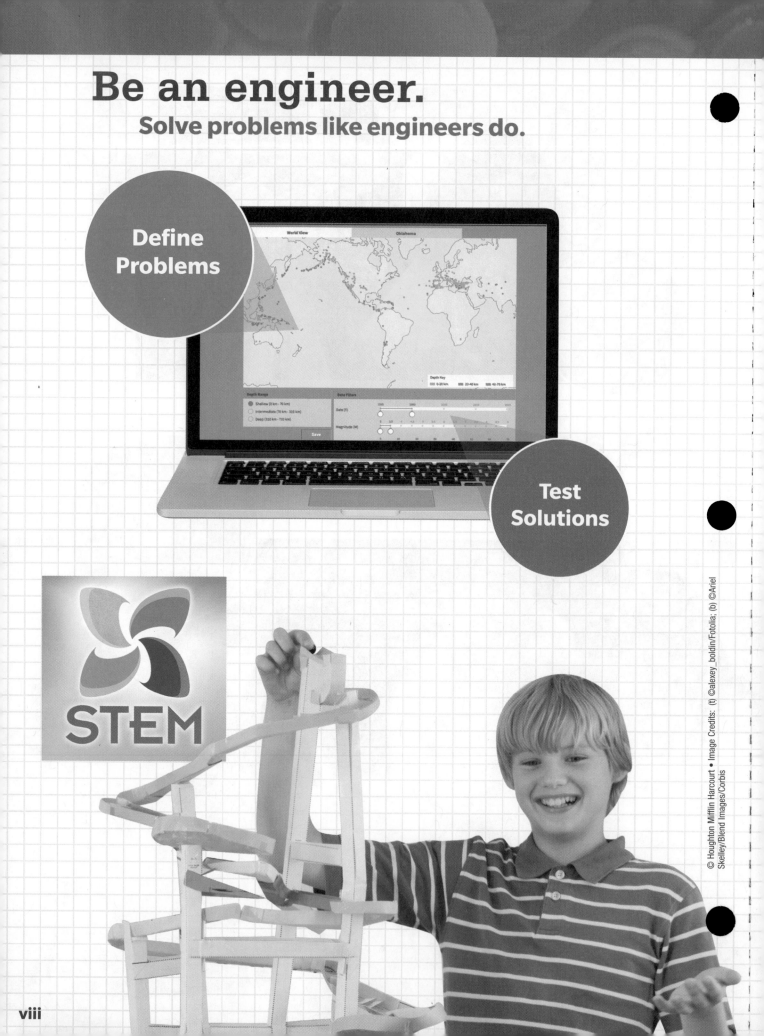

Define Problems

Test Solutions

STEM

Gather Information

Think Critically

Explain your world.
Start by asking questions.

Conduct Investigations

Collaborate

Develop Explanations

Construct Arguments

There's more than one way to the answer. What's YOURS?

YOUR Program

Write-In Book:

- a brand-new and innovative textbook that will guide you through your next generation curriculum, including your hands-on lab program

Interactive Online Student Edition:

- a complete online version of your textbook enriched with videos, interactivities, animations, simulations, and room to enter data, draw, and store your work

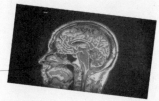

Describing Information Processing in Animals

Animals bodies gather and process information from their environment.

How does an animal's body process information from the environment?

Start typing...

More tools are available online to help you practice and learn science, including:

- **Hands-On Labs**
- **Science and Engineering Practices Handbook**
- **Crosscutting Concepts Handbook**
- **English Language Arts Handbook**
- **Math Handbook**

UNIT 1

Cells

When you look at an object under a microscope, you are able to tell by its appearance whether or not it is a living organism.

© Houghton Mifflin Harcourt • Image Credits: ©Garry DeLong/Oxford Scientific/Getty Images

UNIT 2

Organisms as Systems

© Houghton Mifflin Harcourt • Image Credits: ©Christina L. Evans/Rainbow/RGB Ventures/SuperStock/Alamy

The hard shell of the thorn bug helps it blend in with the plant it lives on, and also provides a protective armor.

Contents

Fraternal twins, like these white-faced marmoset pups, grow from two different fertilized eggs so they are genetically not identical.

© Houghton Mifflin Harcourt • Image Credits: ©blickwinkel/Alamy

Whether you are in the lab or in the field, you are responsible for your own safety and the safety of others. To fulfill these responsibilities and avoid accidents, be aware of the safety of your classmates as well as your own safety at all times. Take your lab work and field work seriously, and behave appropriately. Elements of safety to keep in mind are shown below and on the following pages.

Safety in the Lab

- [ ] Be sure you understand the materials, your procedure, and the safety rules before you start an investigation in the lab.

- [ ] Know where to find and how to use fire extinguishers, eyewash stations, shower stations, and emergency power shut-offs.

- [ ] Use proper safety equipment. Always wear personal protective equipment, such as eye protection and gloves, when setting up labs, during labs, and when cleaning up.

- [ ] Do not begin until your teacher has told you to start. Follow directions.

- [ ] Keep the lab neat and uncluttered. Clean up when you are finished. Report all spills to your teacher immediately. Watch for slip/fall and trip/fall hazards.

- [ ] If you or another student are injured in any way, tell your teacher immediately, even if the injury seems minor.

- [ ] Do not take any food or drink into the lab. Never take any chemicals out of the lab.

Safety in the Field

- [ ] Be sure you understand the goal of your fieldwork and the proper way to carry out the investigation before you begin fieldwork.

- [ ] Use proper safety equipment and personal protective equipment, such as eye protection, that suits the terrain and the weather.

- [ ] Follow directions, including appropriate safety procedures as provided by your teacher.

- [ ] Do not approach or touch wild animals. Do not touch plants unless instructed by your teacher to do so. Leave natural areas as you found them.

- [ ] Stay with your group.

- [ ] Use proper accident procedures, and let your teacher know about a hazard in the environment or an accident immediately, even if the hazard or accident seems minor.

Safety Symbols

To highlight specific types of precautions, the following symbols are used throughout the lab program. Remember that no matter what safety symbols you see within each lab, all safety rules should be followed at all times.

Dress Code

- Wear safety goggles (or safety glasses as appropriate for the activity) at all times in the lab as directed. If chemicals get into your eye, flush your eyes immediately for a minimum of 15 minutes.
- Do not wear contact lenses in the lab.
- Do not look directly at the sun or any intense light source or laser.
- Wear appropriate protective non-latex gloves as directed.
- Wear an apron or lab coat at all times in the lab as directed.
- Tie back long hair, secure loose clothing, and remove loose jewelry. Remove acrylic nails when working with active flames.
- Do not wear open-toed shoes, sandals, or canvas shoes in the lab.

Glassware and Sharp Object Safety

- Do not use chipped or cracked glassware.
- Use heat-resistant glassware for heating or storing hot materials.
- Notify your teacher immediately if a piece of glass breaks.
- Use extreme care when handling any sharp and pointed instruments.
- Do not cut an object while holding the object unsupported in your hands. Place the object on a suitable cutting surface, and always cut in a direction away from your body.

Chemical Safety

- If a chemical gets on your skin, on your clothing, or in your eyes, rinse it immediately for a minimum of 15 minutes (using the shower, faucet, or eyewash station), and alert your teacher.
- Do not clean up spilled chemicals unless your teacher directs you to do so.
- Do not inhale any gas or vapor unless directed to do so by your teacher. If you are instructed to note the odor of a substance, wave the fumes toward your nose with your hand. This is called wafting. Never put your nose close to the source of the odor.
- Handle materials that emit vapors or gases in a well-ventilated area.
- Keep your hands away from your face while you are working on any activity.

Safety Symbols, continued

Electrical Safety

- Do not use equipment with frayed electrical cords or loose plugs.
- Do not use electrical equipment near water or when clothing or hands are wet.
- Hold the plug housing when you plug in or unplug equipment. Do not pull on the cord.
- Use only GFI protected electrical receptacles.

Heating and Fire Safety

- Be aware of any source of flames, sparks, or heat (such as flames, heating coils, or hot plates) before working with any flammable substances.
- Know the location of lab fire extinguisher and fire-safety blankets.
- Know your school's fire-evacuation routes.
- If your clothing catches on fire, walk to the lab shower to put out the fire. Do not run.
- Never leave a hot plate unattended while it is turned on or while it is cooling.
- Use tongs or appropriate insulated holders when handling heated objects.
- Allow all equipment to cool before storing it.

Plant and Animal Safety

- Do not eat any part of a plant.
- Do not pick any wild plant unless your teacher instructs you to do so.
- Handle animals only as your teacher directs.
- Treat animals carefully and respectfully.
- Wash your hands throughly with soap and water after handling any plant or animal.

Cleanup

- Clean all work surfaces and protective equipment as directed by your teacher.
- Dispose of hazardous materials or sharp objects only as directed by your teacher.
- Wash your hands throughly with soap and water before you leave the lab or after any activity.

Student Safety Quiz

Circle the letter of the BEST answer.

1. Before starting an investigation or lab procedure, you should
   A. try an experiment of your own
   B. open all containers and packages
   C. read all directions and make sure you understand them
   D. handle all the equipment to become familiar with it

2. At the end of any activity you should
   A. wash your hands thoroughly with soap and water before leaving the lab
   B. cover your face with your hands
   C. put on your safety goggles
   D. leave hot plates switched on

3. If you get hurt or injured in any way, you should
   A. tell your teacher immediately
   B. find bandages or a first aid kit
   C. go to your principal's office
   D. get help after you finish the lab

4. If your glassware is chipped or broken, you should
   A. use it only for solid materials
   B. give it to your teacher for recycling or disposal
   C. put it back into the storage cabinet
   D. increase the damage so that it is obvious

5. If you have unused chemicals after finishing a procedure, you should
   A. pour them down a sink or drain
   B. mix them all together in a bucket
   C. put them back into their original containers
   D. dispose of them as directed by your teacher

6. If electrical equipment has a frayed cord, you should
   A. unplug the equipment by pulling the cord
   B. let the cord hang over the side of a counter or table
   C. tell your teacher about the problem immediately
   D. wrap tape around the cord to repair it

7. If you need to determine the odor of a chemical or a solution, you should
   A. use your hand to bring fumes from the container to your nose
   B. bring the container under your nose and inhale deeply
   C. tell your teacher immediately
   D. use odor-sensing equipment

8. When working with materials that might fly into the air and hurt someone's eye, you should wear
   A. goggles
   B. an apron
   C. gloves
   D. a hat

9. Before doing experiments involving a heat source, you should know the location of the
   A. door
   B. window
   C. fire extinguisher
   D. overhead lights

10. If you get chemicals in your eye you should
    A. wash your hands immediately
    B. put the lid back on the chemical container
    C. wait to see if your eye becomes irritated
    D. use the eyewash station right away, for a minimum of 15 minutes

Go online to view the Lab Safety Handbook for additional information.

© Houghton Mifflin Harcourt

Cells

By using a microscope, tiny organisms can be seen swimming around in this sample of pond water.

When people look at an organism like a fish, they see the organism as a whole. On a fish, we can observe scales, fins, and eyes. However, if we look more closely with the aid of a microscope, the truth is revealed: all living things are made up of tiny structures called cells. Some living things, such as microscopic plankton found in pond water, are made up of one or several cells. Other living things, such as fish and people, have millions of cells! In this unit, you will investigate how cells function as systems and the ways that cell parts contribute to cell function.

Why It Matters

Here are some questions to consider as you work through the unit. Can you answer any of the questions now? Revisit these questions at the end of the unit to apply what you discover.

Questions	Notes
Can you see all the organisms that live in a water sample?	
What technology could help you see organisms that live in a water sample from a local water source?	
How are types of microorganisms similar and different?	
How can you distinguish between living organisms and nonliving materials in a water sample?	
How can microorganisms in a water sample be used to assess the health of a local water source?	

Unit Starter: Observing Differences in Scale

When you view a living organism with a microscope, you can see cells and their structures, which are not visible to your unaided eye. The photo below shows a cat. The smaller images show different magnifications of the cat's hair—100 times larger than actual size and 400 times larger than actual size. Compare how the appearance changes at different magnifications.

Circle the words that correctly complete the sentences.

When there is no magnification, you can see the entire organism, but you see
more / fewer details of the cat hair. At 400X magnification, you can see
more / fewer details of the hair, but you see more / less of the organism's body.

Go online to download the Unit Project Worksheet to help you plan your project.

Unit Project

Test Water Quality

How healthy is a water source in your community? Choose a local water source, collect samples of the water, and view the samples under a microscope. Work with local authorities to determine the quality of the water. Use the organisms and materials present in the water source to make your conclusions. Provide local authorities with your data and analysis, according to their needs.

The Characteristics of Cells

The human brain is composed of many tiny building blocks. The brain's building blocks are made of cells called neurons.

By the end of this lesson . . .

You will be able to explain how living things are built of tiny structures called cells.

Go online to view the digital version of the Hands-On Lab for this lesson and to download additional lab resources.

CAN YOU EXPLAIN IT?

How do these tiny structures relate to the onion?

The photo on the left shows a magnified image of a single layer of red onion skin.

1. Record your observations of the magnified image and the onion.

2. What do you think is needed in order to observe the tiny structures?

 EVIDENCE NOTEBOOK As you explore the lesson, gather evidence to explain how whole organisms are made up of building blocks, or cells.

Identifying Cells

When you were very young, you may have played with wooden blocks or plastic bricks. You could build almost anything from these blocks or bricks—from an insect to a tree or even a person. But did you know that nature has its own building blocks? All living things are made of these "blocks."

Living Things Are Made of Cells

Living things, including bacteria, mushrooms, mosses, and insects, are called **organisms.** What makes organisms different from nonliving things? One difference is that all organisms are made of one or more cells. A **cell** is the smallest unit that can be said to be alive. Cells are the fundamental units of all living organisms. A human is made up of more than 30 trillion cells!

The aquatic plant *Elodea* on the left is shown without magnification. The images on the right show how the same *Elodea* looks when magnified.

3. What can you see when you look at this plant with your unaided eyes? What do you see when the plant is magnified?

Observe Magnified Objects

These photographs show three different objects as they appear when observed through a microscope. As you explore the images, think about how cells relate to each object.

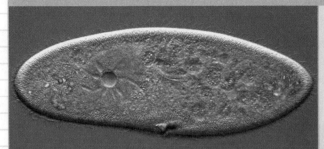

Paramecium A paramecium is an organism made up of a single cell. Tiny hairlike structures, called cilia, surround the cell. The cilia beat back and forth, allowing the paramecium to move through the water where it lives.

Shrimp eye This photo shows thousands of cells that make up a shrimp's eye. Shrimp are able to detect very fast motion because of the arrangement of specialized cells in their eyes.

Pencil tip The tip of this pencil is made of graphite, which is a form of carbon, mixed with clay. This mixture of materials leaves a gray mark on paper, which is easily erased.

4. **Discuss** How do the objects differ from one other?

5. The paramecium is an example of a living / nonliving thing. The shrimp is an example of a living / nonliving thing. The pencil is an example of a living / nonliving thing. The paramecium and the shrimp do / do not contain cells. The pencil does / does not contain cells.

EVIDENCE NOTEBOOK

6. Is the onion shown at the beginning of the lesson an example of a living or nonliving thing? Record your evidence.

Cells Are Building Blocks of Life

Now you know that living things are made of one or more cells and nonliving things are not made of cells. When you look at an object under a microscope, you will be able to tell by its appearance whether it is a living organism. Although all organisms are made of cells, these cells can have different shapes and functions.

Living organisms that are composed of just one cell are called **unicellular** organisms. Examples of unicellular organisms are bacteria, *Paramecia*, and yeasts. Other living organisms that are made of more than one cell are called **multicellular** organisms. All animals and most plants are examples of multicellular organisms.

Analyze Magnified Objects		

7. Label each photo as a unicellular organism, multicellular organism, or nonliving object. Then record your evidence.

	Glucose is a simple sugar made by plants during photosynthesis. Magnified glucose crystals are shown here.	
	This photo shows a magnified cross-section through a salt gland on a crocodile's tongue.	
	Desmids are a type of algae that mainly live in freshwater. The single cell is often divided into two symmetrical halves.	

Cells Come from Existing Cells

New cells can be produced only by existing cells. The cells of a living organism divide to create new cells so that the organism can grow and carry out life processes. When a cell divides, it produces a new cell that is identical to it. New cells help an organism grow and replace cells that are old, weakened, or dead.

Explore ONLINE!

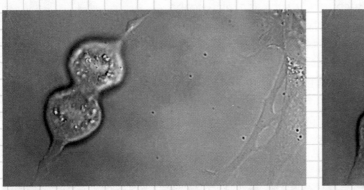

These two images show a cell going through the process of cell division.

8. How are the cells in the photo on the left different from the cells in the photo on the right?

Language SmArts
Summarize Parts of a Theory

The discovery that cells divide to create new, identical cells is part of the cell theory, which has been developed by many scientists over more than a hundred years. The cell theory states that:

- All living organisms are composed of one or more cells.
- Cells are the building blocks of life.
- All cells come only from existing cells.

9. Summarize the three parts of the cell theory in your own words, using examples of organisms that you are familiar with.

_____

_____

_____

_____

_____

_____

Investigating the Scale of Cells

Most cells are too small to see with the unaided eye. Because of their extremely small size, most cells can be observed only by using technology, such as a microscope. A microscope makes a cell and its parts that cannot be observed at one scale visible to humans at another scale.

Today, scientists use several types of microscopes to view cells. For example, light microscopes form images by directing light through one or more lenses. Light microscopes can be used to view living or dead specimens. Electron microscopes form images with a beam of electrons. Electron microscopes can only be used to view dead specimens. However, they can provide much greater magnification than light microscopes, such as seeing details within an individual cell.

10x

100x

A butterfly's wing is made up of thousands of scales, which each grow from a single cell. Here, wing scales are shown at 10 times larger than actual size and 100 times larger than actual size.

10. The butterfly's wing looks different in the different photos because

    A. the photos were taken at different scales.

    B. the wing was bent to reveal its inner structure in the last photo.

    C. one photo shows the edge of the wing and one shows the middle of the wing.

11. The magnified photos show more / less detail of smaller / larger portions of the butterfly wing.

Hands-On Lab
Observe Cells with a Microscope

You will use a microscope to observe living and nonliving materials at different scales.

    Microscopes use lenses to magnify objects. The way that the lenses bend light toward your eyes makes the objects appear larger. The scale on a microscope at which you are viewing an object is called *magnification*.

MATERIALS
- eyedropper
- human hair
- light microscope
- microscope slides with coverslips
- salt
- sand
- thin slice of cork
- tissue paper

Procedure and Analysis

STEP 1 Look at the cork sample. Write your observations in the "No microscope" column of the table.

STEP 2 Put the cork sample on a slide and add a drop of water. Carefully place the coverslip on the slide so that the cork sample is in the middle.

STEP 3 Make sure that the 10x lens of the microscope is in place. Put the prepared slide on the microscope stage.

STEP 4 Look through the microscope's eyepieces. Adjust the position of the lens until the image of the cork is sharp.

STEP 5 Observe the cork. Write your observations in the 10x column of the table.

STEP 6 Now click the 40x lens into place. Use only the fine focus (never the coarse focus) to adjust the image. View the cork sample and write your observations in the 40x column of the table.

STEP 7 Repeat steps 1–6 with the samples of human hair, tissue paper, salt, and sand.

	Observations		
Sample	No microscope	10x	40x
cork			
human hair			
tissue paper			
salt			
sand			

STEP 8 **Do the Math** Think about what you observed using the 10x and 40x lenses. Which magnification allows you to see the greater amount of close-up detail? Were you able to observe cells in any of the objects at this magnification?

STEP 9 **Engineer It** Identify the needs filled by the microscope in this activity. What are the limitations of the microscope you are using?

EVIDENCE NOTEBOOK

12. What does observing different scales of the onion skin tell you about its composition? Record your evidence.

Relate Scale to Observations

Microscopes have different lenses that magnify objects to 10x, 100x, or even larger scales. The scale a scientist chooses to view an object depends on the scientist's goal.

13. The photographs show a images observed at three different scales. For each photo, identify which science career would likely use the scale shown to make observations.

Career	Description
Geneticist	studies the organelles inside a cell, especially those that carry genetic instructions
Primatologist	studies how gorillas behave
Hematologist	studies blood, diseases of the blood, and how blood is produced in the body

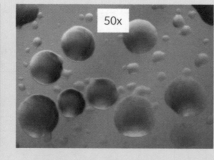
50x

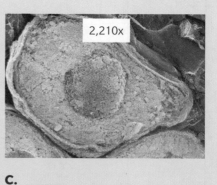
2,210x

A. _____ **B.** _____ **C.** _____

Continue Your Exploration

Name: _____   Date: _____

Check out the path below or go online to choose one of the other paths shown.

Microscopes over Time	• **Hands-On Labs** 🖐 • **Making a Microscope** • **Propose Your Own Path**	*Go online to choose one of these other paths.*

Although glass lenses were used to magnify images for many years, early lenses were not powerful enough to identify individual cells. The invention of the compound microscope in the late 1500s was an early step toward this discovery. Since then, microscopes have come a long way. Today, microscopes allow us to study our world at very small scales.

There are many kinds of microscopes. A compound microscope contains two or more lenses. Total magnification is the product of the magnifying power of each lens. Typically, the magnifying power of a compound microscope is much stronger than that of an individual lens.

Robert Hooke (1635–1703) was an English scientist who built a compound microscope and used it to examine organisms, such as insects and sponges. When he examined thin slices of cork, which is the outer bark of a species of oak tree, he noticed small hollow compartments. Hooke coined the term *cell* while describing the "honey-comb"-like properties of the hollow compartments, which reminded him of rooms in which monks lived. What Hooke actually observed was the cell walls of dead cork cells.

Scientists continued to innovate and modify the microscope over the next 150 years. The designs became sturdier, more lightweight, and easier to use. Microscopes also became capable of greater magnification over time. This evolving technology allowed scientists to ask more and more interesting questions about the characteristics of cells.

Hooke first identified cells using this microscope.

© Houghton Mifflin Harcourt • Image Credits: ©SSPL/Getty Images

Continue Your Exploration

When new technology is developed, scientists often learn new information. You learned on the preceding page that cells were not discovered until the compound light microscope was developed. Now, an electron microscope can make images of individual atoms.

For very small objects, compound light microscopes or electron microscopes can be used. Compound light microscopes use a series of lenses to magnify objects. Electron microscopes use tiny particles called electrons to produce clearer and more detailed images than compound light microscopes. Two types of electron microscopes are scanning electron microscopes and transmission electron microscopes.

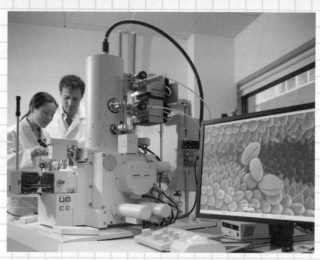

A scanning electron microscope focuses an electron beam over the surface of an object to create an image. The electrons in the beam interact with the object and produce signals that can be used to obtain information about the surface and composition of the object.

1. What is the difference between a compound light microscope and an electron microscope?

2. How did technology contribute to the discovery of cells?

3. **Career/Engineering Connection** As a scientist, what are some questions you could answer with a microscope but not with your eyes alone?

4. **Collaborate** With a classmate, conduct research to compare different kinds of microscopes. Focus on the following: the history and design of compound light microscopes, transmission electron microscopes, and scanning electron microscopes. Choose one and create a diagram to show how it works. Present your diagram to the class.

Can You Explain It?

Name: _____   **Date:** _____

Revisit these two images, one of a group of cells and one of a sliced onion.

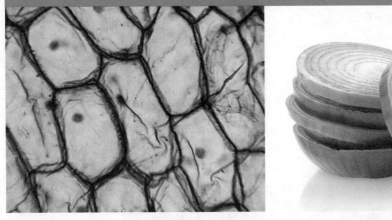

How do these tiny structures relate to the onion?

EVIDENCE NOTEBOOK

Refer to the notes in your Evidence Notebook to help you construct an explanation for how an onion can be built of layers of cells.

1. State your claim. Make sure your claim fully explains how the layers of cells and the onion are related.

2. Summarize the evidence you gathered to support your claim and explain your reasoning.

Checkpoints

Answer the following questions to check your understanding of the lesson.

Use the photograph to answer Questions 3 and 4.

3. This photo shows an organism that is magnified 100 times. This organism is
   unicellular / multicellular.

4. When viewing a rock at a similar magnification, you would / would not see cells.

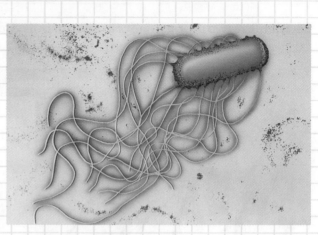

Use the photograph to answer Questions 5–7.

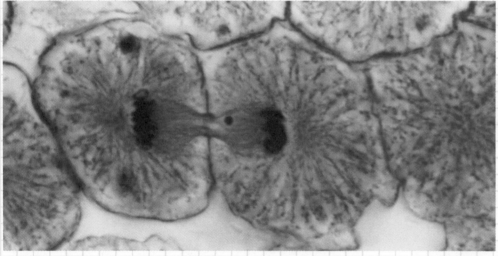

5. The process shown in this photo provides benefits to the organism in which it is occurring. What are they? Select all that apply.

   A. aids reproduction of organism

   B. aids growth of organism's body

   C. aids genetic diversity in organism

   D. aids repair of organism's body

6. The process shown in this photo is called
   cell fusion / cell division / cell scale.

7. The process shown in the photo illustrates that

   A. all of an organism's cells come only from existing cells.

   B. organisms have all the cells they will ever have at birth or germination.

   C. organisms acquire new cells from outside their body.

Interactive Review

Complete this section to review the main concepts of the lesson.

All living things are made of one or more cells. Living things can be unicellular (made of one cell) or multicellular (made of more than one cell). All cells come only from preexisting cells. Cells are the building blocks of life.

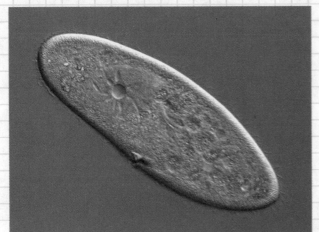

A. You are designing a model that will demonstrate the three parts of the cell theory. Explain how you could demonstrate all three parts.

Microscopes and other technology have allowed scientists to discover the relationship between cells and organisms. Scale is relevant in the study of cells.

B. Explain the scale of cells and the technology that helps us observe them.

Cell Structures and Function

© Houghton Mifflin Harcourt • Image Credits: ©Laguna Design/Oxford Scientific/Getty Images

The structures inside these algal cells perform specific functions that help the cells survive.

By the end of this lesson . . .

you will be able to describe how a cell's functions are performed by specific cell structures.

Go online to view the digital version of the Hands-On Lab for this lesson and to download additional lab resources.

CAN YOU EXPLAIN IT?

How is a cell like a sports stadium?

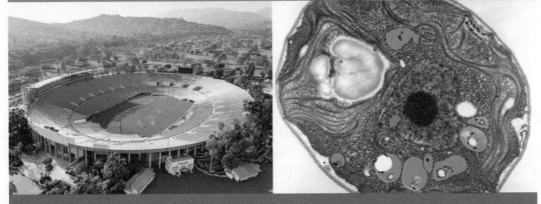

A stadium is a complex system that has specific needs. A cell is also a system that has needs. Like a stadium, a cell must allow substances to enter and leave through its walls. What other needs does a cell have?

It's game day! Across the country, people gather at sports stadiums to watch their favorite sport and cheer on their favorite team. Each sports stadium can be thought of as a system with needs that must be met in order for it to function properly. Walls hold together all the parts of a sports stadium, but objects must be able to move into and out of the stadium as needed. Some objects going into the stadium, such as food items, must move through the walls. Trash moving out of the stadium must also move through the walls. Doors in the walls of the stadium allow objects to enter and leave the stadium. These are two ways that the needs of the stadium system are met.

1. Did you ever think about a stadium as a complete system? What parts of the stadium system provide the functions it needs?

2. What are some functions that a cell and a sports stadium have in common?

EVIDENCE NOTEBOOK As you explore the lesson, gather evidence to help explain how a cell's functions are performed by specific cell structures.

Comparing Cell Structures

A Cell Is a Whole System

Cells make up all living organisms, including both unicellular organisms and multicellular organisms. In a unicellular organism, the cell must perform all of the functions it needs to live. In a multicellular organism, different types of cells perform unique functions to provide for the needs of the whole organism. For example, the skin cells of your body provide protection from harmful substances in the environment. Your red blood cells carry oxygen to all cells in the body.

However, regardless of their function or the type of organism they compose, all cells have similar basic functions they need to carry out to remain alive. These functions are carried out not by the cell as a whole, but by specific parts of the cell. Cells store and process information. Cells gather energy and matter from the environment. Cells use energy to carry out functions. Cells get rid of wastes.

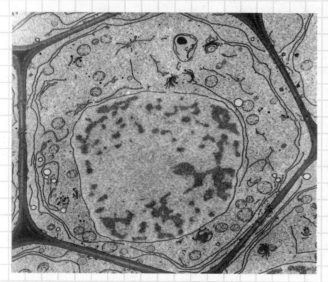

This plant cell is from the root tip of a type of corn.

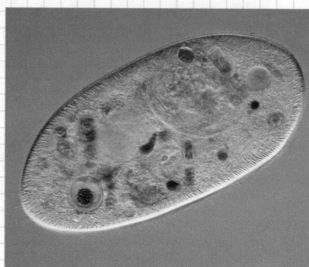

This animal cell is a small single-celled organism called a protozoan.

3. **Discuss** Compare and contrast the plant cell and the animal cell. How are they similar? How are they different? What basic functions do both of them share?

Types of Cells and Their Structures

All cells have three structures that carry out essential life functions. The **cell membrane** surrounds and protects the cell. The cell membrane allows only certain substances, such as nutrients, into the cell and certain other substances, such as wastes, out of the cell. *Cytoplasm* is a liquid substance that fills the inside of the cell and supports cell structures. Genetic material contains all the information a cell needs to function.

Many cells also contain **organelles,** small membrane-bound structures in the cytoplasm that are specialized to perform a specific function. Mitochondria, chloroplasts, and ribosomes are examples of organelles. Not every cell contains every type of organelle, and different types of cells may have additional kinds of organelles. Although many kinds of cells exist, all cells can be organized into two categories: prokaryotes and eukaryotes.

Prokaryotic Cells

A prokaryotic cell contains its genetic material in the cytoplasm. Most prokaryotic cells do not have any membrane-bound organelles, although they do have structures called ribosomes that make proteins. Prokaryotic cells are unicellular organisms. Bacteria are the largest group of prokaryotes.

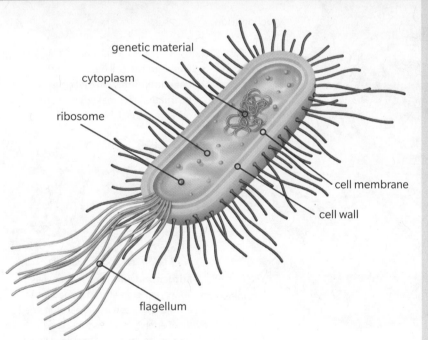

Prokaryotic Cell

genetic material
cytoplasm
ribosome
cell membrane
cell wall
flagellum

genetic material Genetic material contains information that directs all of the cell's functions.

cytoplasm The cytoplasm surrounds and supports organelles inside the cell.

ribosome Ribosomes make proteins inside the cytoplasm.

cell membrane The cell membrane surrounds and protects the cell and controls what materials go into and out of it.

cell wall The cell wall provides structural support for plant cells and some prokaryotic cells.

flagellum These projections move the prokaryote through its environment.

4. Which structure controls what goes into and out of the cell? Explain in your own words why this function is important to the function of a cell as a whole.

Eukaryotic Cells

Eukaryotic cells are generally larger and more complex than prokaryotic cells. In a eukaryotic cell, genetic material is enclosed in a membrane-bound organelle called the **nucleus.** Eukaryotic cells also have additional membrane-bound organelles.

Animals and plants are both made of eukaryotic cells. Both have organelles called **mitochondria,** which convert the energy stored in food to a form of energy that cells can use. Plant cells and animal cells also have some different structures. For example, plants make their own food using a process called *photosynthesis*. Therefore, plant cells have organelles called **chloroplasts,** where photosynthesis occurs. Animals do not make their own food, so animal cells do not have chloroplasts. Plant cells also have a rigid **cell wall** that supports the cell. The extra support of a cell wall isn't needed in animal cells, because most animals have some type of skeleton that supports the body.

Animal Cell

An animal cell has some of the same structures as a prokaryotic cell, such as a cell membrane and cytoplasm, and some different structures.

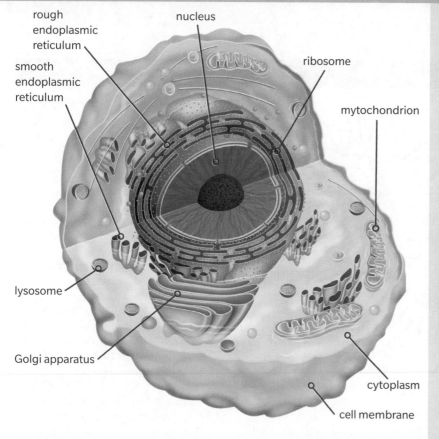

rough endoplasmic reticulum
nucleus
smooth endoplasmic reticulum
ribosome
mytochondrion
lysosome
Golgi apparatus
cytoplasm
cell membrane

Nucleus The cell nucleus contains genetic information that gives instructions for making proteins and other materials the cell needs.

Mitochondrion These organelles convert energy stored in food into a form the cell can use. Cells that need a lot of energy, such as muscle cells, have more mitochondria than do cells that need less energy, such as nerve cells.

Rough ER The rough ER is located near the nucleus and contains ribosomes on its surface. It is involved in making and processing proteins.

Smooth ER The smooth ER does not contain ribosomes. It makes fat-based molecules called lipids that are used to make membranes.

Golgi apparatus The Golgi apparatus takes proteins from the ER and moves them to different parts of the cell.

Lysosome These structures contain powerful chemicals known as enzymes that break down food.

© Houghton Mifflin Harcourt • Image Credits: (t)©London School of Hygiene & Tropical Medicine/Science Source; (b)©CNRI/Science Photo Library/Getty Images

Plant Cell

In addition to a cell membrane, cytoplasm, nucleus, and mitochondria, a plant cell also has a cell wall and chloroplasts.

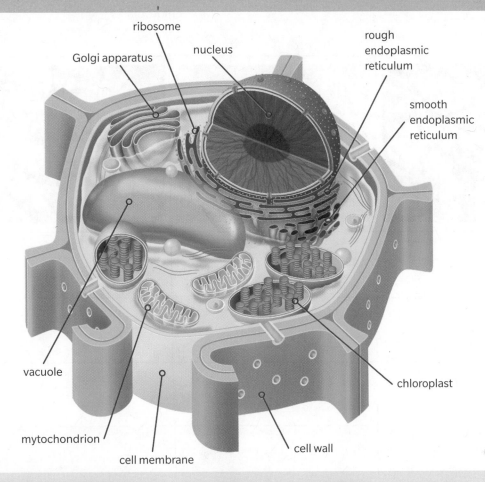

- Golgi apparatus
- ribosome
- nucleus
- rough endoplasmic reticulum
- smooth endoplasmic reticulum
- vacuole
- chloroplast
- mytochondrion
- cell membrane
- cell wall

Chloroplast In the cells of plants and a few other kinds of organisms, chloroplasts capture energy from sunlight and change it into food that stores energy for the cell to use.

Cell wall A cell wall surrounds the entire plant cell, including its cell membrane, and supports the plant cell. Most bacterial cells, which are prokaryotic, also have cell walls.

Vacuole A large central vacuole is bound by a membrane and contains materials and waste. It also maintains adequate pressure inside the plant cell.

5. Read these cell observations. In the space next to each answer choice, write whether the cells described are prokaryotic cells, animal cells, plant cells, or there is not enough information to determine.

   A. Cell has a membrane and ribosomes. _____

   B. Cell has many chloroplasts. _____

   C. Cell has a cell membrane and mitochondria, but no cell wall. _____

   D. Cell has a nucleus. _____

   E. Cell has a nucleus and cell wall. _____

Identify Differences Between Cells

6. Fill in the table to indicate which cell structures belong to which cells.

cell membrane
cell wall
chloroplasts

mitochondria
nucleus

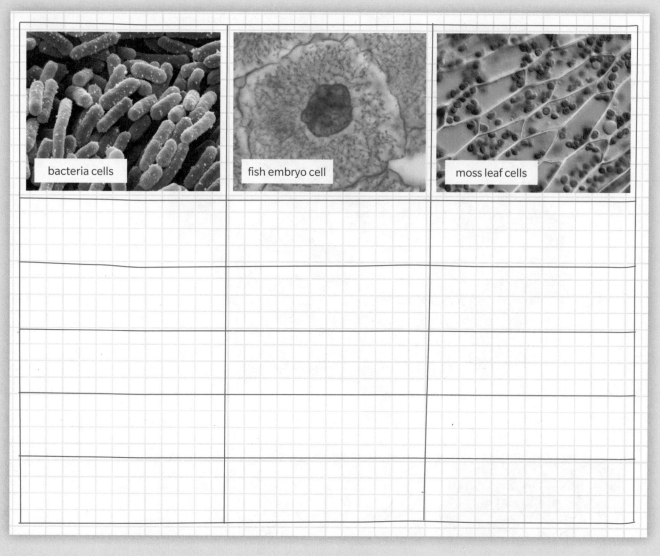

bacteria cells

fish embryo cell

moss leaf cells

7. How do moss leaves and fish differ? How are they the same?

_____
_____
_____
_____
_____
_____
_____
_____
_____

Using Cell Models

Imagine that a friend asks you how the sizes of planets in our solar system compare to each other. A map of the solar system would show you the planets and the shapes of their orbits, but it would be difficult to see how their sizes compare. However, if you built a model of the solar system, you could show your friend many things about the solar system. You could show planet sizes in relation to each other, to the sun, and in general how far away the planets are from each other.

In this example, a three-dimensional (3D) model helped to explain relationships between the planets. You can use 3D models to visualize and explore many structures and systems, especially systems that are very large or very small.

Scientists use models for many reasons. For example, models can show objects or processes that are too small or that happen too slowly or too rapidly to see with the unaided eye. Scientists use both two-dimensional (2D) and 3D models to study cells. Examples of a 2D cell model are an illustration or a photograph. Examples of a 3D cell model are a physical model, which can be touched and moved around, or a computer model, which can be manipulated digitally. 3D models are useful in exploring and understanding the relationships among the parts of a cell.

WORD BANK

nucleus
cell membrane
mitochrondria
chloroplasts

8. An analogy is a model of a relationship. Look at each organelle and read the analogy of its function. Then use the word bank to label each organelle.

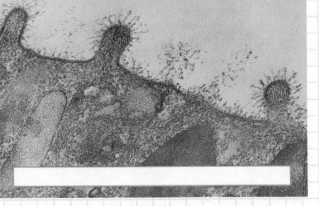

Analogy: Border between countries

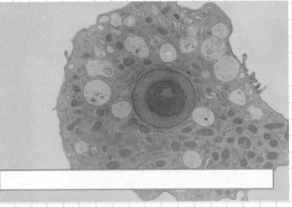

Analogy: Control center

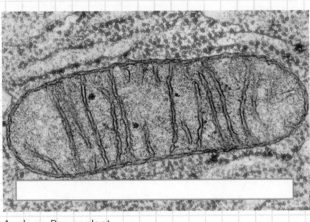

Analogy: Power plant

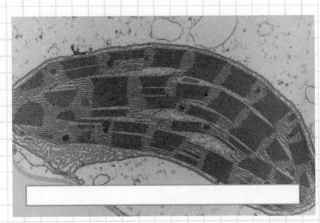

Analogy: Solar panel

Hands-On Lab
Use Cell Models to Investigate Cell Size

How can you predict the impact of cell size on cell function? Use large and small cubes of gelatin to model cell function in cells of different sizes. Use evidence to support an explanation of how cell size affects function.

The gelatin cubes that you will work with represent a model of a cell. Using a cube allows you to easily calculate its dimensions, such as its surface area and volume. A cell's surface area-to-volume ratio is an important factor in its functioning.

MATERIALS
- 250 mL beakers (2)
- calculator (if desired)
- 473 mL containers, plastic (2)
- gelatin cubes, prepared (1 large and 27 small)
- ruler, metric
- stopwatch or clock with second hand
- warm water

Procedure and Analysis

STEP 1 Work with a partner. Measure the length of each side of the large gelatin cube and one of the smaller cubes. (All of the smaller cubes are the same size.) Record the measurements in the data table.

	Cube sides (cm)	Surface area (cm²)	Volume (cm³)	SA:V ratio	Time to dissolve
Large cube					
Smaller cubes					

STEP 2 Place the large cube in one of the plastic containers. Place the 27 smaller cubes in the other container.

STEP 3 Ask your teacher to fill your beakers with warm water to the same level. Then pour the water from the beakers into both plastic containers at the same time. Make sure all the gelatin cubes are submerged in the water. Start the timer. If any water has spilled, clean it up immediately to avoid slips.

STEP 4 **Do the Math** While you wait for the cubes to dissolve, calculate the surface area, volume, and surface area-to-volume ratio for the large cube and the smaller cubes. Enter this data into the data table.

To calculate the surface area (SA) of a cube, first multiply the cube's length (L) by its width (W). Then multiply the answer by 6 (for the 6 sides of the cube).

Formula: SA = L × W × 6

To calculate the volume (V) of the cube, multiply the length (L) by the width (W) by the height (H).

Formula: V = L × W × H

A ratio compares two quantities. One way to write the surface area-to-volume ratio is to use a colon between the surface area (SA) and the volume (V).

SA to V ratio = SA : V

STEP 5 Record the length of time it took for the gelatin cubes to completely dissolve.

STEP 6 Which of the cubes has the largest total surface area and the largest total volume? Which has the highest surface area-to-volume ratio?

STEP 7 Describe the relationship between surface area-to-volume ratio and the rate it took for the cubes to dissolve.

STEP 8 Remember that all cells must take in materials and get rid of wastes through the cell membrane. Think about how the surface area-to-volume ratio affected the time it took for the different-sized cubes to dissolve. What can you infer about how the surface area-to-volume ratio of a cell would affect the movement of materials into and out of a cell?

Evaluate Cell Models

9. There are advantages and disadvantages to each type of model. Examine the 2D and 3D cell models, note the types of information each provides, and list the pros and cons of using each model.

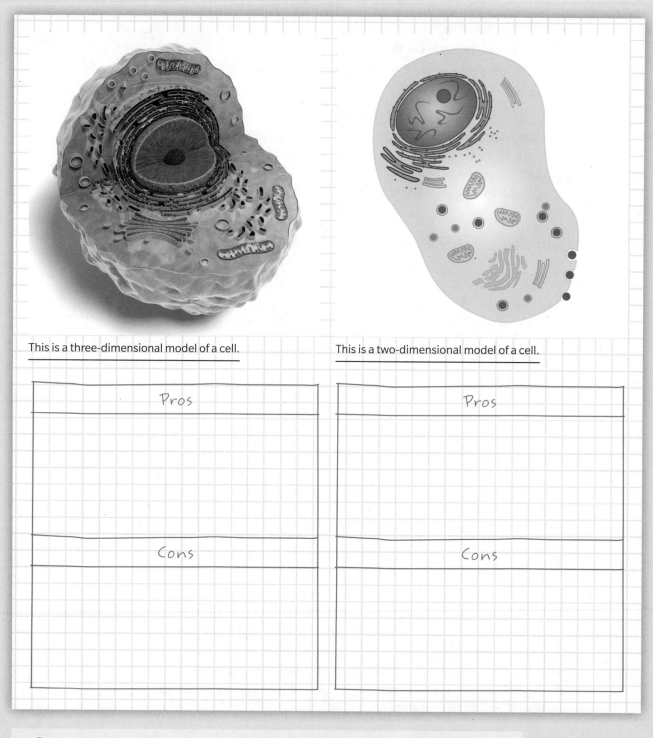

This is a three-dimensional model of a cell.

Pros
Cons

This is a two-dimensional model of a cell.

Pros
Cons

 EVIDENCE NOTEBOOK

10. Does the 3D model enhance your understanding of how cell structures work together to allow the functioning of the cell as a whole? Record your observations and evidence.

Explaining Limits to Cell Size

Imagine you are looking at a small mouse. You know that both the mouse and your own body are made of cells because cells are the building blocks of life. Cell sizes can vary based on their function. For example, red blood cells that needs to transport blood throughout your body are small. But, muscle cells in your leg are much larger. A human contains more than 37 trillion cells. Given how much larger you are compared to a mouse, how do your cells compare in size? Would you expect the mouse to have smaller cells than you do, or fewer cells than you do?

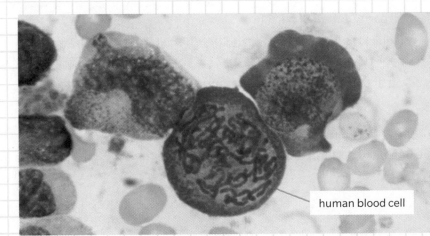

This purple human red blood cell is roughly 6-8 µm. One micron, or 1 µm, is 1/1,000 the size of 1mm.

human blood cell

11. Humans must have *bigger cells / more cells* than mice.

12. Given your answer, explain your reasoning for the difference in cell size or number between humans and mice.

Relationship Between Surface Area and Volume

Scientists have observed that the sizes of the same cell types of a human and a mouse are approximately the same size. While some cells can grow larger than other cells, there is a limit to how large a cell can grow. The reason has to do with a cell's surface area-to-volume ratio. A cell's surface area is the total area of its outer surface. Its volume is the amount of space inside the cell. Recall that all materials that enter and exit a cell must pass through its cell membrane. As a cell gets larger, the greater its volume is in relation to its surface area. Because a cell is small and has a small internal volume in relation to its surface area, materials are able to rapidly move through its cell membrane quickly. But there is a limit to how quickly these materials can pass through the cell membrane. If a cell is too big, wastes cannot properly exit the cell and nutrients cannot enter it quickly enough to fuel cell processes.

13. While a sports stadium is a system much like a cell is, it does not have the same limits on size that cells do. Record evidence to support how a cell's size is more important for transporting material across its surface.

Relate Structure of Cell Membrane to Cell Size

14. What problems might result if a cell gets too large? Circle all that apply.

   A. Wastes will not be able to leave the cell quickly enough.

   B. Nutrients will not be able to reach all parts of the cell quickly.

   C. Nutrients will move into the cell too quickly for the cell to use and then harm the cell.

   D. Wastes will leave the cell so quickly that they will take necessary nutrients with them.

 15. **Language SmArts** Citing evidence from the text and from your calculations, explain why cells are unable to perform important functions if they become too large.

_____

_____

_____

_____

_____

_____

_____

_____

 16. **Engineer It** You are designing a building that must minimize energy transfer in the form of heat loss. Describe a building shape that you think would minimize heat loss through the surface of the building, and explain how that shape relates to the surface area-to-volume ratio.

_____

_____

_____

_____

_____

_____

_____

_____

Continue Your Exploration

Name: _____   Date: _____

Check out the path below or go online to choose one of the other paths shown.

People in Science

- **Hands-on Labs**
- **Understanding Cell Metabolism**
- **Propose Your Own Path**

Go online to choose one of these other paths.

Lynn Margulis, Biologist

Lynn Margulis (1938–2011) was a biologist who made many important contributions to science. Her most well-known contribution was her proposal in 1966 that eukaryotic cells evolved from the process of endosymbiosis. She proposed that billions of years ago smaller prokaryotes began living inside larger host prokaryotic cells. In some cases, smaller prokaryotes entered larger cells as parasites. In others, smaller cells were engulfed by larger cells. Margulis proposed that mitochondria and chloroplasts of today's eukaryotic cells are descended from free-living bacteria.

Eventually Margulis outlined her ideas in her 1970 book *Origin of Eukaryotic Cells.* Most scientists of the time were skeptical of the ideas because they thought the organelles of eukaryotic cells evolved from materials found inside the cells.

Today, most scientists accept Margulis's hypothesis. She and other scientists showed that, like a cell nucleus, mitochondria and chloroplasts contain DNA. Also, the DNA of mitochondria and chloroplasts is different from the DNA in a cell's nucleus. Instead, the DNA of mitochondria and chloroplasts resembles the DNA of bacteria.

American biologist Lynn Margulis at work in a greenhouse, circa 1990.

© Houghton Mifflin Harcourt • Image Credits: ©Nancy R. Schiff/Archive Photos/Getty Images

Continue Your Exploration

1. Which statements provide evidence to support Lynn Margulis's hypothesis of endosymbiosis? Arrange the statements below into the order that accurately shows the sequence of events described in Margulis's hypothesis by writing the number 1, 2, 3, or 4 next to each statement.

_____ Prokaryotes inside other prokaryotes evolved into organelles.

_____ Prokaryotes lived inside other prokaryotes in a symbiotic relationship.

_____ Prokaryotes that had engulfed other prokaryotes evolved into eukaryotes.

_____ Free-living prokaryotes engulfed other free-living prokaryotes.

2. How do the findings of Margulis and other scientists—that mitochondria and chloroplasts have their own DNA, like a cell's nucleus—support the hypothesis of endosymbiosis?

3. Explain how Lynn Margulis's hypothesis changed scientific ideas about cell development.

4. **Collaborate** Work with another classmate to discuss why Lynn Margulis's career is important to science and to diversity in science. Present your ideas to the class.

© Houghton Mifflin Harcourt

Can You Explain It?

Name: _____ **Date:** _____

Recall ways in which a cell and a stadium are both systems.

How is a cell like a sports stadium?

EVIDENCE NOTEBOOK

Refer to the notes in your Evidence Notebook to help you construct an explanation for how a cell is like a sports stadium.

1. State your claim. Make sure your claim fully explains how a cell could be like a sports stadium.

2. Summarize the evidence you have gathered to support your claim and explain your reasoning.

Checkpoints

Answer the following questions to check your understanding of the lesson.

Use the photograph to answer Question 3.

3. Study the photograph. Which of the following describes this cell? Select as many as apply.

   A. animal cell

   B. plant cell

   C. prokaryotic

   D. eukaryotic

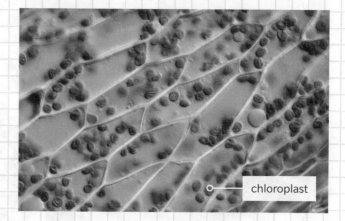
chloroplast

4. If a cell's surface area-to-volume ratio increased from 3:1 to 4:1, what impact would that have on the transport of materials across the cell membrane?

   A. it would be unchanged

   B. transport would increase

   C. transport would decrease

   D. none of the above

Use the illustration to answer Questions 5 and 6.

5. What is the function of the structure marked A in the illustration below?

   A. process nutrients

   B. make proteins

   C. store wastes

   D. hold genetic information

6. Based on what you know of the function of the structure labeled A, select the best analogy of its function.

   A. allow system to function properly

   B. build system structure

   C. dispose of system wastes

   D. consume food

A

Interactive Review

Complete this section to review the main concepts of the lesson.

All cells contain specialized structures that perform necessary functions within the cell.

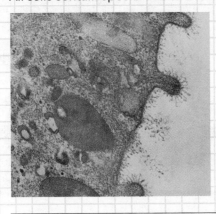

A. Relate the following structures within a cell to their function: nucleus, chloroplast, mitochondria, cell membrane, cell wall

Examining 3D models of cells can enhance understanding of how cell structures work together to maximize function.

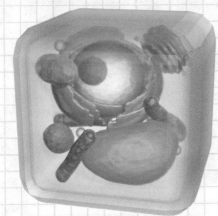

B. Explain how using 3D models of cells can help scientists gain a better understanding of cell structures and function.

A cell's surface area-to-volume ratio determines how large a cell can be while still performing necessary functions.

C. Describe the relationship between a cell's surface area-to-volume ratio and the transport of wastes from inside the cell to the outside environment.

Choose one of the activities to explore how this unit connects to other topics.

Physical Science Connection

Scanning / Transmission Electron Microscopes
In order to examine the smallest parts of cells in detail, scientists can use a scanning electron microscope or a transmission electron microscope. These types of microscopes use beams of electrons, rather than light.

Using library or Internet resources, research how scanning electron microscopes (SEM) and transmission electron microscopes (TEM) work. Investigate the advantages and disadvantages of both types of microscopes. Compare what is visible in a cell with a light microscope versus what is visible in a cell with an SEM or TEM. Create a multimedia presentation with your findings to share with the class.

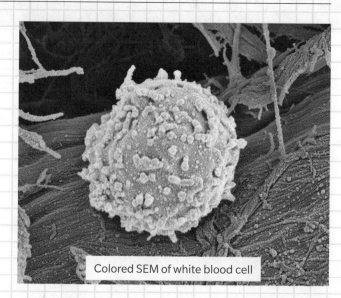
Colored SEM of white blood cell

Art Connection

Making Art of the Invisible World Compound light microscopes allow us to see cells at a scale that is not possible with our unaided eyes. Some artists make observations using microscopes to produce models for drawings, sculptures, and other artworks.

View a cell under a light microscope and use the image as a model for a work of art that you create, such as a drawing, painting, collage, or sculpture. If you are not able to view a cell under a microscope, search online for images of cells under microscopes to use as models for your artwork. Present your artwork to the class and explain the type of cell and its parts.

Computer artwork based on nerve cell and DNA

Health Connection

Pollution, Cancer, and the Cell Environmental pollutants in the air, water, and soil can cause cancer in living organisms. Cancer is a class of diseases characterized by uncontrolled cell growth and division. Cancer cells often have mechanisms that help them resist destruction by the immune system.

Using library or Internet resources, investigate a pollutant that is associated with a certain type of cancer. Research how that type of cancer affects living cells and how scientists and doctors are working to counteract cancer. Share your research with the class as a multimedia presentation.

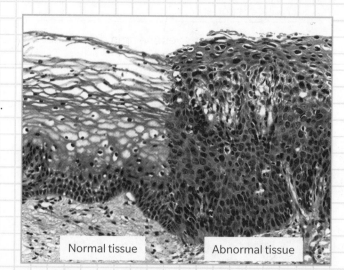
Normal tissue   Abnormal tissue

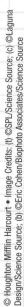

Name: _____ Date: _____

Complete this review to check your understanding of the unit.

Use the photograph to answer Questions 1–2.

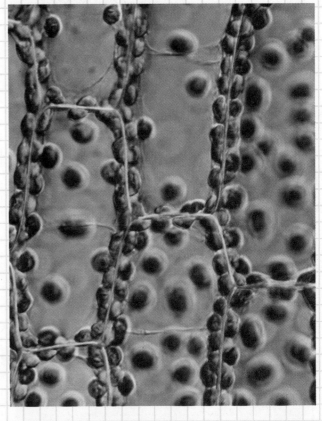

1. What can you tell about this object from the photo? Select all that apply.

   A. It is a living organism.

   B. It is a nonliving thing.

   C. It is unicellular.

   D. It is multicellular.

   E. It is a plant.

   F. It is an animal.

2. Which of the following statements are evidence that support your answer to question 1? Select all that apply.

   A. Cells are visible.

   B. Cells are not visible.

   C. Only one cell is visible.

   D. More than one cell is visible.

   E. Cell walls are visible.

   F. Chloroplasts are visible.

Use the cell diagram to answer Questions 3–4.

3. Which of the following statements provide evidence that the cell in the diagram is a eukaryote? Select all that apply.

   A. The cell has a nucleus.

   B. The cell does not have a nucleus.

   C. The cell has membrane-bound organelles.

   D. The cell does not have membrane-bound organelles.

4. This cell is a(n) plant / animal cell, because it does not have chloroplasts / mitochondria or a cell membrane / wall.

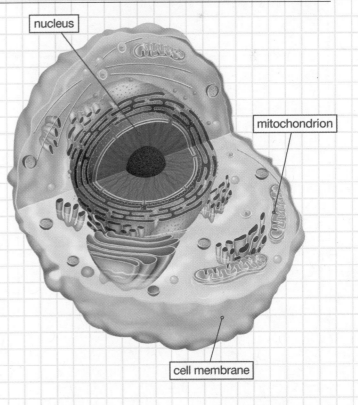

nucleus

mitochondrion

cell membrane

Name: _____ **Date:** _____

5. Complete the table by adding information for each cell structure listed. Describe
what type(s) of cells have each structure, how many of each structure are present in a
cell, and the function of each structure in the cell.

Cell Structure	Cell Type	Quantity	Function
Nucleus			
Cell Membrane			
Chloroplast			
Mitochondria			

© Houghton Mifflin Harcourt

Use the photo to answer Questions 6–10.

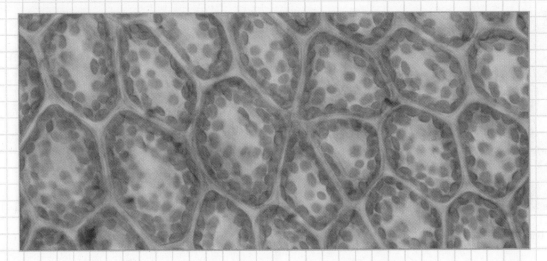

6. Analyze the photo that shows cells from a living organism. Are these plant or animal cells? Which cell structures are present to justify your claim?

7. If you were examining this organism without magnification by using your unaided eye, explain how it would affect your observation of the cell.

8. How would these cells appear under a microscope at a higher magnification? What parts of the cells would be visible?

9. How would these cells appear at a lower magnification? What parts of the cells would be visible?

10. How does observing an organism at different magnifications help scientists?

Use the image to answer Questions 11–13.

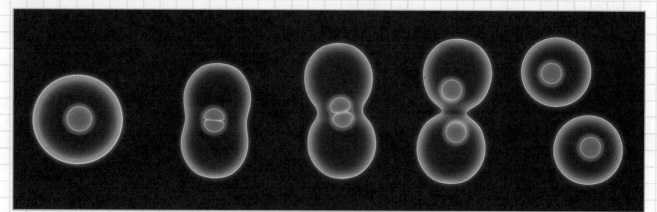

11. What part of the cell theory does this image illustrate?

12. Before the invention of microscopes, would it have been possible for scientists to observe the phenomenon shown in the image? Why or why not?

13. Scientists often use models to study cells. What are the pros and cons of using a 3D model, rather than a 2D model, to study the phenomenon shown in the image?

© Houghton Mifflin Harcourt • Image Credits: ©Ramona Kaulitzki/Panther Media/age fotostock

Name: _____ **Date:** _____

How can doctors explain what sickle cell anemia is to affected children?

The doctors at a local hospital have noticed that their youngest sickle cell anemia patients are having difficulty understanding their diagnosis. Your team has been assembled to construct an educational campaign geared toward children age 10 and under. First, you need to explain what cells are. Next, you need to describe red blood cells and their importance. Then you need to explain what sickle cell anemia is, using 2D or 3D models. Models should show a normal red blood cell and a blood cell of a person with sickle cell anemia. Use the image below to help your team construct the models.

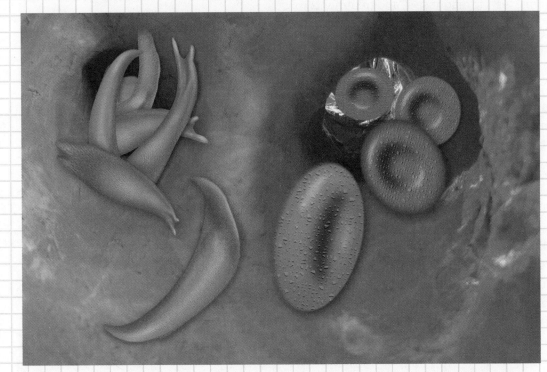

The steps below will help guide your research and develop your recommendation.

1. **Define the Problem** With your team, write a statement defining the problem you have been asked to solve. What are the criteria and constraints in developing this educational campaign?

2. **Construct an Explanation** Using what you have learned in this unit, construct an explanation of what cells are. Make sure the explanation can be understood by children age 10 and under.

3. **Conduct Research** Do research on human blood, including its function and structure, as well as the function of different components that make up blood.

4. **Conduct Research** Do research on sickle cell anemia. Find out about its risk factors, causes, symptoms, tests to diagnose it, and treatments.

5. **Construct Models** Using what you have learned about red blood cells and about sickle cell anemia, construct two models: one of a normal red blood cell and one of a red blood cell twisted into a sickle shape. The models may be 2D or 3D, depending on what materials are available.

6. **Design and Communicate a Solution** Put together a presentation, aimed at children age 10 and under who have sickle cell anemia, that doctors could use to educate young patients about their diagnosis. The presentation should include your explanation of what cells are, your research on red blood cells and sickle cell anemia, and your models of a normal red blood cell and an affected red blood cell. Give your presentation to your class.

✓ **Self-Check**

	I defined the problem of creating an educational campaign about sickle cell anemia for children age 10 and under who have the disease.
	I explained what cells are in a way that young children can understand and investigated the importance of the different components of human blood, including red blood cells.
	I researched the risk factors, causes, symptoms, diagnostic tests, and treatments for sickle cell anemia.
	I constructed two models: one of a normal red blood cell and one of an affected red blood cell.
	I created a presentation about sickle cell anemia for young patients.

Organisms as Systems

This Venus flytrap has tiny hairs covering the inside of its leaves. When a fly bumps the hairs, the leaves close shut. Then the plant releases enzymes to digest the fly.

Organisms have a wide range of responses to their environments. These responses are made possible through the cooperation of body systems. Scientists study body systems and other levels of organization to understand how they function and how they help organisms sense their environment. In this unit, you will investigate the relationship between structure and function at each level of organization, and how survival needs of organisms are accomplished by systems working together.

Why It Matters

Here are some questions to consider as you work through the unit. Can you answer any of the questions now? Revisit these questions at the end of the unit to apply what you discover.

Questions	Notes
What happens to an organism if an organ or organ system does not function properly?	
Why do organisms forget some things and remember others?	
What factors are involved in memory retention?	
Why do some animals have a heightened sense, such as sight or smell?	
Do organisms instinctively know how to respond to the environment, or do they have to learn how to respond?	

Unit Starter: Understanding Systems Analysis

A cell is the simplest level of organization in an organism. Just like the organism as a whole, a cell is a system. The image below depicts a plant cell and its parts. Explore the picture for more information about the cell as a system.

The cell wall gives the plant cell structure and support.

Chloroplasts are the organelles that produce energy for the cell through photosynthesis.

The cell membrane surrounds and protects the cell.

Nutrients enter the cell through the cell wall and cell membrane.

Waste products leave the cell through the cell membrane and cell wall.

1. In this plant cell, the system boundary is the cell wall / cell membrane. The system inputs are nutrients / wastes and the outputs are nutrients / wastes. An example of a system process is chloroplasts / photosynthesis.

Go online to download the Unit Project Worksheet to help you plan your project.

Unit Project

Causes of Organisms' Behaviors

Why do organisms behave the way they do? Plan an investigation into the unusual behavior of an organism and the body systems involved that will help explain how the organism responds to stimuli.

© Houghton Mifflin Harcourt

Levels of Organization in Organisms

The hard shell of the thorn bug helps it blend in with the plant it lives on, and also provides a protective armor.

By the end of this lesson . . .

you will be able to relate structure to function at each level in an organism.

Go online to view the digital version of the Hands-On Lab for this lesson and to download additional lab resources.

CAN YOU EXPLAIN IT?

How can systems with such different structures perform the same function?

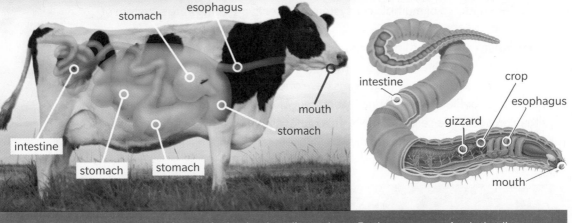

Cows are animals that eat grass, hay, and other hard-to-digest plants. Earthworms are animals that live in soil and eat decaying plant and animal matter.

1. The cow's digestive system and the worm's digestive system both break down food, but they do not look the same. Compare and contrast the two systems. What explanation can you suggest to explain the similarities and differences between the two digestive systems?

 EVIDENCE NOTEBOOK As you explore the lesson, gather evidence to help you explain the structures of the two digestive systems.

Exploring Levels of Organization in Organisms

Unicellular and Multicellular Organisms

Every living thing is a system that performs all the processes needed for survival. Some living things are made up of multiple subsystems. Other living things are a system of only a single cell.

An **organism** is a living thing made up of one or more cells that can perform all the processes needed for life. Organisms that are made up of a single cell are called *unicellular* organisms. Unicellular organisms have one level of organization. All the functions needed for life are performed by one cell. *Multicellular* organisms are made up of more than one cell. The cells that make up a multicellular organism are specialized and organized to perform specific functions. Multicellular organisms have more than one level of organization.

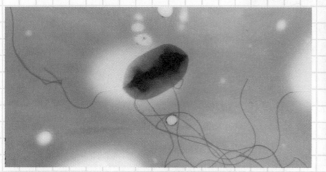

E. coli bacteria are unicellular. They have whip-like structures that help them move and attach to host cells.

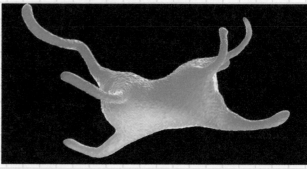

A protozoan is unicellular. This *Amoeba proteus* moves and engulfs prey using extensions of its body.

Oak trees are multicellular. They have many leaves to capture sunlight, and a specialized stem called a *trunk*.

The Eurasian water shrew is multicellular. It uses its sensitive whiskers to hunt snails and aquatic insects underwater.

2. **Discuss** Multicellular organisms can be made up of billions of cells. How do you think having specialized cells is an advantage for a multicellular organism?

Analyze Levels of Organization in a Lizard

When this frilled lizard is threatened, its heart rate increases in preparation to fight or to run away. The lizard stands on its back legs, hisses, and expands the large skin flap that surrounds its neck.

Cardiac muscle cells are specialized for contraction. The structure of protein fibers in the cell allows it to stretch and contract.

Cardiac muscle cells branch and connect to each other to form cardiac muscle tissue. Special junctions where the cells connect allow all the cells in the tissue to contract at the same time.

The heart is an organ in the circulatory system. The many cells stretching and contracting together make the heart stretch and contract, pumping blood as it changes shape.

3. Is the frilled lizard unicellular or multicellular? Use evidence to explain your answer.

4. Describe the relationship between a cardiac muscle cell and the frilled lizard's heart.

From Cells to Organisms

All organisms are made of cells. Each cell type is specialized for its particular job. For example, cells lining the lungs of some animals have tiny, hair-like extensions that trap particles that the animal breathes in. These cells form a **tissue,** a group of similar cells that work together to perform a function. This tissue lining the lungs moves the trapped particles out of the lungs by the coordinated movement of the hair-like structures on each individual cell. The lungs of the animal are organs. An **organ** is made up of two or more tissues that carry out a specialized function of the body. The lung contains muscle and connective tissues that expand and contract the lung during breathing. The lungs are part of an **organ system,** a group of organs and other structures that work together to perform specific body functions. The lungs, nose, and throat, are organs in the animal's respiratory system.

5. Match the terms to the levels of organization in the plant by writing in the appropriate blank space.

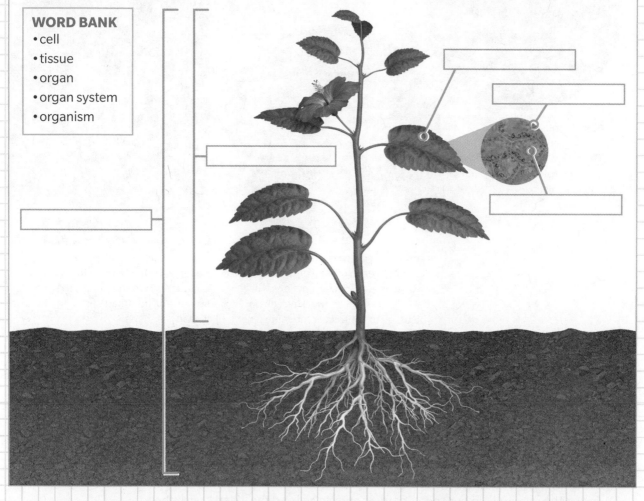

WORD BANK
- cell
- tissue
- organ
- organ system
- organism

6. Plants are multicellular organisms with a root system and a shoot system. Would you expect the cells that make up root tissue to look similar to or different from the cells in the leaf tissue? Explain your answer.

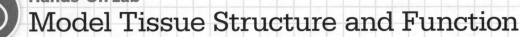

Model Tissue Structure and Function

You will model two different tissue types and relate their structure to their function.

Stick out your tongue and feel the surface. Now, feel the bones in your fingers and the skin on the back of your hand. Do you think all of these structures are made of the same tissue, or are they different?

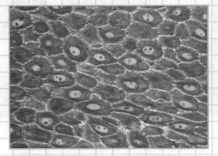

This tissue protects the skin from abrasion. It can be especially thick on the heels of your feet.

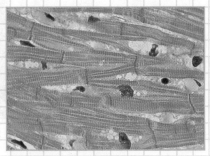

This tissue is located in the heart. It stretches and contracts to make the heart pump blood.

MATERIALS
- adhesive putty
- beads
- cardboard
- construction paper
- foam peanuts
- glue
- markers
- modeling clay
- pompoms
- rice
- rubber bands
- scissors
- sponges
- tape

Procedure and Analysis

STEP 1 Look at the tissues in the photographs. Record your observations about the structure and shape of the cells.

STEP 2 Choose the materials that you think will best model the cells and how they are connected. Create your model.

STEP 3 Which materials did you use to make your models? Why did you choose them?

STEP 4 How do you think the structures of these tissues relate to their function?

7. The gizzard in the earthworm contains small stones that help grind up bits of food. Why might the earthworm have a gizzard but the cow does not? Record your evidence.

Do the Math | Analyze Size and Scale in Organisms

Have you ever wondered how many cells are in your body? Biologists use a unit of measure called a nanogram (ng) to measure the mass of cells and other microscopic structures. There are 1 billion, or 10^9, nanograms in 1 gram.

This hedgehog is being weighed before his winter sleep.

8. If the average mass of a cell is 1 nanogram, approximately how many cells are in the body of a hedgehog that weighs 400 grams?

   STEP 1 Convert 400 grams to nanograms.

   $$400 \text{ g} \times \frac{10^9 \text{ ng}}{1 \text{g}} = \boxed{} \text{ ng}$$

   STEP 2 Use the ratio $\frac{1 \text{ cell}}{1 \text{ ng}}$ to find the number of cells in the body of the hedgehog.

   $$\boxed{} \text{ ng} \times \frac{1 \text{ cell}}{1 \text{ ng}} = \boxed{} \text{ cells}$$

9. The pancreas is an organ that is part of the digestive system. The hedgehog's pancreas has a mass of 4 grams. What percent of the hedgehog's total mass is the mass of the pancreas?

   STEP 1 Write the ratio of the mass of the pancreas to the total mass of the hedgehog.

   $$\frac{4 \text{ g (pancreas)}}{400 \text{ g (total mass)}} = \boxed{}$$

   STEP 2 Multiply by 100 to convert to percent.

   $$\boxed{} \times 100 = \boxed{} \%$$

Categorize a Level of Organization

10. **Discuss** Blood is made up of blood cells suspended in a liquid matrix called *plasma*. Blood contains red blood cells, white blood cells, and platelets. All of these cell types originate in the bone marrow. The blood provides all the cells in the body with oxygen, helps regulate body temperature, and helps the body fight infection. With a partner, discuss whether or not you think blood is a tissue, a fluid, or both. Support your argument with evidence.

_____

_____

_____

Relating Structure to Function in Living Things

Think of an object or tool that you use every day, such as a pencil or water bottle. There is a relationship between the structure and function of these objects. The pencil is long and thin, so it's easy to hold. The water bottle has a hollow space to hold liquid, and a smooth lip to drink from. Structure-function relationships exist at all levels of organization in an organism the same way.

Structure and Function of Cells and Tissues

All organisms are made of cells, but not all cells are the same. Cells are fit for the job they perform. For example, cells that engulf harmful particles in the body are flexible and can take any shape. But cells that form a protective barrier, such as the cells that cover a plant stem, are stiff and regularly shaped. A tissue has characteristics similar to the cell type that it is made of.

Structure and Function of Animal Tissues

Explore the photograph of the rat tissues to see how the structure relates to function.

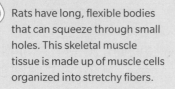

Rats have long, flexible bodies that can squeeze through small holes. This skeletal muscle tissue is made up of muscle cells organized into stretchy fibers.

Rats are omnivores and will eat just about anything they can find. The tissue that lines the rat intestine has finger-like projections that increase the surface area.

Rats can remember food sources. The cells that make up the nervous tissue have long, branching extensions.

11. The tissue that lines the intestine helps release / **absorb** / break down nutrients by increasing the intestinal surface area. The long extensions of nervous tissue **connect** / ingest / destroy the cells in the brain and other parts of the body. The muscle cells are organized into flexible fibers because muscle tissue elongates and absorbs / protects / **contracts**.

Structure and Function of Organs

Just as the structure of a cell or tissue relates to its function, the structure of an organ relates to the function it performs. For example, some organs are shaped like hollow tubes to transport materials, such as the vessels that carry blood throughout your body. Others are sac-like to hold materials, such as your stomach that stores food and your lungs that expand to hold air.

Tulip flowers are organs that contain the structures the plant uses to reproduce. They come in a wide variety of shapes and colors.

12. Look at the photo of the tulip. Record your observations about the structures of the organs in the tulip shoot system.

Organ	Structural Observations	Functions
stem		transports nutrients and stores water, supports plant
leaf		captures sunlight for making nutrients, regulates water loss
flower		attracts animal pollinators

13. **Draw** The leaves of the tulip are adapted to grow in full sunlight conditions. How do you think the leaves of a low-light plant might look? Draw your leaves and support your prediction by comparing them to the tulip leaves.

Structure and Function of Organ Systems

Most organisms have organ systems that perform specialized functions. For example, a respiratory system is an animal organ system that takes in oxygen and releases carbon dioxide. Some animals that do not have a respiratory system simply exchange these gases through their skin. Animals that have a more complex respiratory system are able to exchange gases more effectively because specialized organs are working together.

air sacs

lung

This scarlet macaw is a South American parrot that can be seen flying above the rainforest canopy.

14. Birds have an organ system that is very efficient at transferring oxygen to all parts of the bird's body. Why do you think birds need to maximize oxygen efficiency?

15. Birds have air sacs and lungs. When birds breathe in / out, oxygen-rich air fills the lungs and air sacs. When birds breathe in / out, the oxygen-poor air leaves the lungs, and stored fresh air enters the lungs from the air sacs. This means that birds always have a supply of oxygen- rich / poor air.

Language SmArts

Analyze Structure and Function of Bird Bones

16. Unlike other animals that have solid bones, a bird's bones are hollow. Bird bones connect directly to the bird's air sacs, so they can be filled with air. Write an explanation of how the structure of bird bones relates to the function of flight.

_____

_____

_____

_____

_____

_____

_____

_____

_____

Analyzing Body System Interactions

Body Systems Interact to Perform Functions

Organisms need to process nutrients and take in oxygen. They need to move to find food and mates, avoid predators, and travel to warmer temperatures. In multicellular organisms, body systems work with other body systems to perform functions. The coordination of systems gives an organism a greater variety of possible functions and responses.

Sailfish are the fastest fish in the ocean. They travel to the Gulf of Mexico from January to March to feed on sardines.

17. Look at the photo of the sailfish and the sardines. Think about what these organisms need, and how they respond to their environment. Record your ideas in the table.

Need	Response
food	
	swim faster
warm up	
	travel to different location

 EVIDENCE NOTEBOOK

18. In the cow, food travels through four different stomach compartments so that it can be fully broken down. What factor do you think contributes to the structure of the cow's digestive system? Record your evidence.

Human Body Systems

19. When you perform an activity, which organ systems are involved? Look at the photographs of people involved in different activities. Decide which organ systems are working together to perform the function shown.

The **circulatory system** delivers nutrients and oxygen to all cells in the body. It carries carbon dioxide and other waste products away from the cells.

The **respiratory system** takes in oxygen and releases carbon dioxide as we breathe.

The **muscular system** moves bones, causes the heart to beat, and moves food through the digestive system.

The **skeletal system** supports the body, protects organs, allows movement, and makes blood cells.

The **nervous system** controls body movement and coordinates communication between the brain and the environment.

The **digestive system** breaks down food into essential nutrients and expels solid waste from the body.

The **excretory system** removes liquid wastes from the body.

A. The muscular / digestive and excretory / skeletal systems allow the arms to move, spinning the wheels of this bike.

B. The respiratory/excretory and nervous/circulatory systems allow this student to breathe and read music.

C. Body functions slow down as you sleep, but they do not stop! For example, the digestive / excretory system continues to break down food, and the muscular / circulatory system continues to deliver nutrients throughout the body.

20. The hummingbird is performing multiple activities. Choose an activity that you see and record two body systems that you think are working together to produce the activity.

This hummingbird's wings beat more than 50 times per second!

Engineer It

Compare Natural and Designed Systems

Humans use an industrial process to digest plant matter for use in products, such as paper. The papermaking process begins by feeding wood chips cut from trees into a tall, cylindrical tower that has multiple cooking chambers. The cooking process uses chemicals, heat, and pressure to break down the fibers in the wood to make a material called *pulp*. After passing through all the cooking chambers, the pulp is sent to a washer to wash away the cooking liquid. The pulp is spread out on a screen where it is bleached and dried. The pulp is then cut, stacked, and ready for processing into paper.

This pulp slurry will eventually be made into paper for newsprint.

21. What need does the plant digester fill? How does this compare to the need that an animal's digestive system fills?

_____

_____

_____

22. Make a diagram that shows the steps of making paper into pulp. How do you think this process compares to the digestion of food by animals?

Continue Your Exploration

Name: _____   Date: _____

Check out the path below or go online to choose one of the other paths shown.

Biomimicry

- **Hands-On Labs** ✋
- **Engineering Organs and Tissues**
- **Propose Your Own Path**

Go online to choose one of these other paths.

No matter what you want to do with a machine or process, there is a good chance that there is an organism that does it naturally. *Biomimicry,* or *biomimetics,* uses design solutions found in nature to solve human design problems. For example, researchers are always looking for ways to make a strong yet flexible fiber. One of the strongest known materials is spider silk. Scientists study spider webs to find out what the silk is made of. If researchers could synthesize natural spider silk, it could be used in a wide range of applications. Surgery sutures and wound covers, artificial ligaments and tendons, protective clothing, and fishing nets are some examples of the possibilities.

1. Why do you think more scientists today are turning to nature to solve engineering and design problems? Select all that apply.

   A. Clean and sustainable design solutions could help solve environmental issues, such as pollution.

   B. Scientists are running out of ideas for design and engineering solutions.

   C. Greater understanding of the natural world has led to the discovery of new possibilities for design solutions.

The silk of spiders is incredibly strong, lightweight, and flexible. Scientists hope the silk will replace human-made materials that are not as strong, not as flexible—and not as environmentally friendly.

Continue Your Exploration

Scientists have discovered that brittle stars are covered in thousands of microscopic lenses that may help them avoid predators. These lenses transmit light more perfectly than any human-made lens.

The biomimetic lenses based on the brittle star lens structure are soft, providing better fine-tuning and complexity than conventional hard lenses. The microlenses shown here are part of a devise that is used in digital cameras.

2. Engineers often use designs that mimic shapes found in nature, such as flippers, wings, and beaks. Construct an argument that supports the use of structure-function relationships found in nature in engineering and design. Use the examples as evidence.

3. Sustainability experts help communities, companies, and governments adopt operating practices that are environmentally friendly. They seek to reduce pollution and waste and to increase recycling of resources. How might sustainability experts apply biomimicry to their field?

4. **Collaborate** Brainstorm about animal characteristics that you think could be used to solve human engineering and design problems. Make sketches of your ideas and write explanations to go with them. Present your ideas to the class.

Can You Explain It?

Name: **Date:**

Study the cow and earthworm digestive systems again.

How can systems with such different structures perform the same function?

EVIDENCE NOTEBOOK
Refer to the notes in your Evidence Notebook to help you construct an explanation for why these systems have different structures.

1. State your claim. Make sure your claim fully explains the similarities and differences between the two systems.

2. Summarize the evidence you have gathered to support your claim and explain your reasoning.

© Houghton Mifflin Harcourt • Image Credits: ©Cindy Singleton/iStockPhoto.com

Checkpoints

Answer the following questions to check your understanding of the lesson.

Study the diagram of the kidney to answer questions 3–4.

3. Each kidney contains more than 1 million filtering structures called *nephrons*. The nephron is made up of several tissue types. Based on the information, which statement is true?

   A. The nephron can be defined as an organ.

   B. The nephron cannot be defined as an organ.

   C. The nephron can be defined as an organ system.

   D. The nephron can be defined as a tissue.

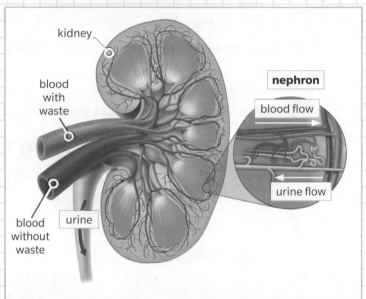

4. Kidneys are organs in the urinary system that remove waste products from the blood. The urinary system is a subsystem of the excretory / digestive system. The urinary system works with the circulatory / digestive system to remove liquid waste from the body.

Use the photograph of the plant to answer questions 5–6.

5. The underground portion of this plant is an example of a(n) tissue / organ system. The branching network of individual cells / organs maximizes the amount of water and nutrients that can be taken up from the soil.

6. What level of organization is a single leaf of this plant?

   A. cell

   B. tissue

   C. organ

   D. organ system

Interactive Review

Complete this section to review the main concepts of the lesson.

Cells, tissues, organs, and organ systems are the levels of organization in living things.

A. How does having multiple levels of organization benefit a multicellular organism?

A relationship exists between structure and function.

B. Describe how structure is related to function in an organism.

Body systems work together to perform all the functions necessary for the survival of an organism.

C. Explain why the failure of one organ or organ system can affect the function of other body systems in an organism.

Plant Bodies as Systems

These tropical plants grow near Arenal Volcano in Costa Rica.

By the end of this lesson . . .

you will be able to evaluate how the survival needs of plants are met by systems working together.

Go online to view the digital version of the Hands-On Lab for this lesson and to download additional lab resources.

CAN YOU EXPLAIN IT?

How can the onyanga thrive in the harsh conditions of the Namib Desert?

The onyanga grows in the Namib desert, where there is little rain but regular, dense fog develops at night.

For many hundreds of years—and possibly even thousands of years—this plant has been growing where not much else can grow. It has only two ragged and torn leaves, a stem, and roots. It may not look like much, but it can go without rain for up to 5 years. The largest onyanga plants are estimated to be nearly 2,500 years old!

1. Why do you think this plant is able to grow in an environment where few other plants can survive?

EVIDENCE NOTEBOOK As you explore the lesson, gather evidence to help you explain how the onyanga's body systems help it survive.

Exploring Plant Body Systems

Plants live on every continent on Earth. They live in places such as lush forests and expansive grasslands. They also live in places you might not expect, such as dry deserts and frozen tundra. They range in size from the tallest giant sequoia trees, reaching more than 80 meters, to the smallest flowering plant, which can fit on the tip of your finger.

All plants are multicellular. They are also eukaryotes—their cells contain membrane-bound organelles, including a nucleus that contains the cell's genetic information. All plants have cell walls and large vacuoles. Most plants convert sunlight to energy by a process called *photosynthesis*.

This maple tree has a central stem, called a *trunk*, that connects the roots to the branches of the tree.

The root system of the saguaro cactus is shallow, but it reaches out as far as the plant is tall.

The water lily's broad, flat leaves float on the water to maximize the amount of sunlight they can capture.

2. **Discuss** With a partner, gather information from the text and the photos to compare the plants shown above. Record your observations in the table.

Similarities	Differences

The Plant Body System

Plants can be divided into two major groups based on the structure and function of their body systems. Most of the land plants on Earth today have a vascular system. A *vascular system* transports materials and provides support to the plant body. Plants that have a vascular system are called *vascular plants*. Plants that do not have a vascular system are called *nonvascular plants*.

Plant Cells

Like all living things, plants are made of cells. Plant cells have rigid cell walls, which help to provide structure and support for the plant.

cell

Plant Tissues

The cells in a plant are organized into three tissue types. Dermal tissue protects the plant, vascular tissue transports materials, and ground tissue provides support and storage.

tissue

Plant Organs

Leaves, stems, roots, and flowers are all plant organs made up of the three tissue types. For example, the stem is covered by dermal tissue. Inside the stem, the vascular tissue that transports water and nutrients is surrounded by ground tissue. Ground tissue gives the stem support and stores materials.

organ

Plant Organ Systems

Plant organs are organized into two organ systems. The *shoot system* includes the leaves, stems, and flowers. The *root system* takes up water and nutrients from the soil. These two systems work together to deliver water and nutrients to the entire plant.

organ system

3. How do you think the leaves of a plant get water? Gather information from the text and the image to help you think about the flow of water in a plant.

EVIDENCE NOTEBOOK

4. The onyanga has a wide, shallow root system. How might this type of root system help the onyanga collect nightly fog? Record your evidence.

Analyze a Plant Body System

Sundews live in habitats where sunlight and water are plentiful but the soil has few nutrients. Like most plants, sundews make their own food using energy from sunlight. Unlike most plants, sundews also capture and eat insects. Sundew leaves are covered with tentacle-like structures that contain a sweet, sticky substance. Insects attracted to the sundew for a tasty meal get trapped in the leaf and are digested by the plant.

When an insect lands on a sundew, it gets stuck on the sticky leaf. The leaf curls around the trapped insect and it is digested by the plant.

Explore ONLINE!

5. Why do you think sundews need to capture insects?

   A. The sundew is unable to make enough food.

   B. The insects provide water to the plant.

   C. The sundew is protecting itself from insects.

   D. The insects provide nutrients that are missing from the soil.

6. Sundews have weak roots. Why do you think sundews do not need strong roots?

_____

_____

_____

_____

7. How does the structure of the sundew leaf relate to its function?

_____

_____

_____

_____

_____

Describing How Plant Systems Process Nutrients

Plants bodies are systems that perform all the processes needed for a plant to live. Plants need sunlight, water, and carbon dioxide to make and transport the food they use as fuel. They also need oxygen to convert the food to energy that is used by all parts of the plant. Nutrients from the soil, such as nitrogen and phosphorus, are used for cellular processes and growth. All of these processes produce unwanted products, so plants also need to get rid of wastes to stay healthy.

Making Food

Like you, plants need food that cells can use for energy. But unlike you, plants do not get their food by eating. Instead, plants make their own food by the process of photosynthesis. *Photosynthesis* is the process that uses energy from sunlight to convert water molecules and carbon dioxide into sugars and oxygen. A **leaf** is the plant organ that is the main site of photosynthesis. The sugars produced in leaf cells are transported from the leaves to all parts of the plant's body.

Inputs and Outputs of Photosynthesis

8. Complete the diagram by labeling the inputs and outputs of the process of photosynthesis. Use evidence from the text.

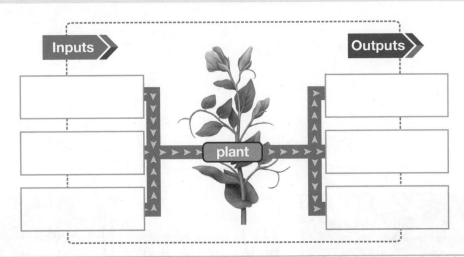

9. Engineer It Solar cells are devices that collect energy from sunlight and convert it into electricity. What plant structure might engineers look at when they are designing the way that solar cells are arranged?

Moving Materials

Materials move through a plant through two kinds of vascular tissue—xylem and phloem. Water and dissolved nutrients enter the plant through the **roots**, organs that absorb water and dissolved nutrients from soil. Roots also anchor the plant in the ground. Roots connect to **stems**, organs that transport nutrients to all parts of the plant body and provide support to the plant. Water moves from the roots to the stems through tube-shaped cells in the xylem tissue. Sugars made during photosynthesis move throughout the plant in the phloem.

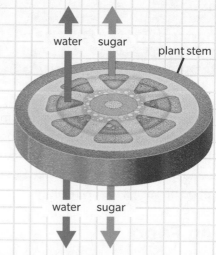

water   sugar

plant stem

water   sugar

Compare Root Systems

10. Using the word bank, complete the Venn diagram by entering the functions you think best describe the root systems.

- absorbs nutrients
- stores nutrients
- drought tolerant
- absorbs water
- anchors plant
- protects soil

taproot   both   fibrous root

taproot

Some plants have a root system called a taproot. As you can see in the photo, these plants have one large main root structure with many smaller branch roots. Taproots can grow deep into the soil.

fibrous root

Other plants have a fibrous root system, in which many branching roots grow close to the soil surface. Fibrous roots can spread wide and form mats that anchor the plant very firmly in the soil.

Hands-On Lab
Observe Transport

You will compare and contrast the movement of water through the stems of two different types of plants.

Procedure

STEP 1 Fill two 16 oz cups with 100 mL of water each. Add 10–15 drops of red food coloring and mix thoroughly.

STEP 2 Use the knife to cut 8 cm sections of the broccoli stem and the asparagus spears. Be sure to cut the stems horizontally.

STEP 3 Place one or two pieces of broccoli stem in one cup and one or two pieces of asparagus spears in the other cup. Be sure the stems stand upright in the water and will not fall over.

STEP 4 Allow the stems to sit in the water for 24 hours. Cut your stems at 1–2 cm intervals to see how far the water traveled up the stems.

STEP 5 Record your observations in the data table below.

Asparagus	Broccoli

Analysis

STEP 6 How do your observations from this activity provide evidence for the function of a plant's vascular system?

STEP 7 Through which vascular tissue did the water move in the broccoli and asparagus stems?

© Houghton Mifflin Harcourt

Disposing of Wastes

Plants produce waste as a result of cell processes, such as photosynthesis. Water, carbon dioxide, and oxygen enter and exit a plant through tiny openings in the leaf surface, called stomata (*sing.* stoma).

Plants also need to get rid of unwanted substances that may enter their systems through water. Some plants store wastes in living cells, such as leaves. These unwanted materials are removed when the leaves fall from the plant.

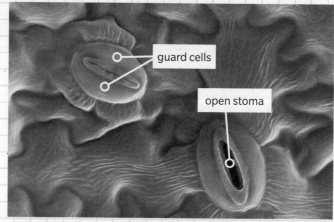

The size, shape, and placement of stomata allow water and gases to efficiently move in and out of the plant.

11. A plant system must balance its need for water with its need for carbon dioxide and oxygen. If too much water is lost, the stomata will close. How does this affect a plant's ability to regulate levels of carbon dioxide and oxygen?

12. **Discuss** What would likely occur if most of a plant's stomata became blocked? Explain your reasoning.

Language SmArts
Use Observations to Develop an Argument

13. This plant has shallow roots, short stems, and leaves that are covered in fuzzy hairs. In what type of environmental conditions might this plant live? Use your observations as evidence to support your argument.

_____

_____

_____

_____

_____

_____

_____

Describing How Plant Systems Respond to the Environment

Unlike many animals, plants cannot move to a new place when their environment changes. Plant bodies respond to a variety of environmental factors. Many of these responses happen very slowly. Other responses are lightning fast! The Venus flytrap will respond to the touch of an insect in a few seconds by snapping its leaf shut. Two factors that plants respond to are light and water.

14. Why do you think it is important for plants to be able to regulate the level of water in their bodies?

Regulating Water

Plants regulate the water in their bodies in response to environmental conditions. Plants regulate water in their bodies mostly by opening and closing their stomata. Two guard cells control the opening and closing of each stoma. When stomata are open, water vapor exits the leaf. Plants can regulate water in other ways also. Some plant leaves have a waxy coating that helps prevent water loss. Plants may also store water in their stems, leaves, or roots.

Do the Math

Calculate Stomata Density

The density of stomata on a leaf surface can be calculated using the equation:

$$\text{Stomatal density} = \frac{S}{S+E} \times 100$$

where S = the number of stomata and E = the number of epidermis cells, which form the outer layer of a leaf.

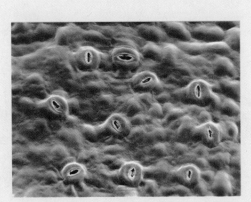

Look at the photo of the leaf.

15. Count and write the number of open stomata that you can see. _____

16. If the number of epidermis cells is 150, what is the density of stomata in this area of the leaf?

17. Stomata density on a particular plant can change depending on environmental conditions. What environmental factors might influence the density of stomata? Explain your thinking.

18. The onyanga opens its stomata only at night. Do you think the onyanga has many or few stomata on the surface of its leaves? Record your evidence.

Responding to Light

Have you ever noticed your houseplant growing toward the window? One way that plants respond to their environment is by growing toward a light source. This process is called *phototropism*. Chemical messengers build up on the shaded side of the plant's stem. These messengers cause the cells to grow longer. As the cells on the shaded side grow longer, they cause the stem to bend toward the light source.

19. What advantage do you think growing toward a light source gives a plant?

Construct an Explanation

20. **Discuss** With a partner, discuss what you think causes a plant to wilt. In your answer, discuss the organs and organ systems involved. Support your answer with evidence.

 Explore ONLINE!

_____

_____

_____

_____

_____

_____

_____

_____

Continue Your Exploration

Name: _____   Date: _____

Check out the path below or go online to choose one of the other paths shown.

Growing Plants in Space

- Hands-On Labs ✋
- Feeding the World Using Less Water
- Propose Your Own Path

Go online to choose one of these other paths.

The International Space Station is a research laboratory that travels at a speed of 8 km per second and orbits Earth every 90 minutes. Solar panels provide power to the station, and life support systems supply oxygen and remove unwanted gases from the enclosed space. The water supply is supplemented by capturing and recycling the water vapors that enter the cabin when the crew members exhale and sweat! The crew members are researching ways to grow food on the space station in the hopes that they will be able to have fresh food available for extended periods of time in space.

An astronaut harvests red romaine lettuce. These plants were grown from seed in the station's plant growth chamber.

Continue Your Exploration

1. One way that plants respond to their environment is by growing in response to gravity, or gravitropism. Roots grow toward the direction of the gravitational pull (downwards). Stems grow opposite to the gravitational pull (upwards). The force of gravity is very weak on the space station, a condition referred to as microgravity. How might microgravity affect the growth of plants on the space station? Select all that apply.

   A. The length and shape of the roots and stems of the plants grown in space might be different than the same plants grown on Earth.

   B. The plant may not be able to absorb and transport water and nutrients in microgravity.

   C. The plant would not be able to respond to light in microgravity.

2. One of the biggest challenges of long-term space travel is having a sufficient supply of fresh water. Water must be recycled and used sparingly to ensure that the crew will have enough water to drink and to bathe. What types of plants from Earth would be good candidates for food plants for the crew of the space station? Select all that apply.

   A. plants from dense areas of vegetation that are adapted to growing in small spaces

   B. plants from dry areas that are adapted to drought conditions

   C. plants from shady areas that are adapted to very little light

3. Do you think the plants on the space station are able to conduct photosynthesis? Explain why or why not.

4. **Collaborate** Collaborate to learn about studies that have been conducted about plant growth in space. You may also find out more about the space garden on the International Space Station. Describe the evidence that researchers have gathered or are gathering to help answer their questions. Collaborate to define a question that you would like to answer about plant growth in space. Describe the evidence you would need to have to answer your question.

Can You Explain It?

Name: _____   **Date:** _____

Think back to the onyanga, the long-lived, two-leaved plant that can survive for years without rain.

How can the onyanga thrive in the harsh conditions of the Namib Desert?

 EVIDENCE NOTEBOOK
Refer to the notes in your Evidence Notebook to help you construct an explanation of how the onyanga can survive in the Namib Desert.

1. State your claim. Make sure your claim fully explains the organs and organ systems involved in the functions that allow the onyanga to survive.

2. Summarize the evidence you have gathered to support your claim and explain your reasoning.

Checkpoints

Answer the following questions to check your understanding of the lesson.

Use the illustration to answer question 3.

3. What would happen if the leaves of the plant shown in the illustration were eaten by an animal? Select all that apply.

   A. The roots would not have a source of energy.

   B. The plant cells would not have a source of energy.

   C. The plant would not be able to regulate water.

   D. The shoot system would not have a source of food.

4. In a season of above average rainfall, a plant would likely respond by *opening / closing* stomata to *store / release* water.

Use the photo to answer questions 5 and 6.

This red mangrove tree has specialized roots, called pop roots, that extend above the ground.

5. The specialized roots of the mangrove tree help the tree to *anchor / float* in the sandy soil. The aboveground portions deliver *oxygen / sunlight* to the roots that are under the water.

6. Mangrove trees live in saline conditions that would kill most other types of plants. How do you think the mangrove tree is able to tolerate this environment?

   A. The mangrove tree needs more salt than other plants to live.

   B. The mangrove tree disposes of salt through its leaves.

   C. Animals that live on the tree eat the salt from the tree.

   D. The mangrove tree does not grow as well as trees that do not live in salty conditions.

Interactive Review

Complete this section to review the main concepts of the lesson.

Plant bodies are made up of cells that form tissues, organs, and organ systems.

A. Describe why the interaction of the different levels of organization in the plant body are needed for the plant body system to function.

Plant bodies are systems that perform all the functions needed by the plant to live.

B. Draw Make a diagram to explain how a plant's root system and shoot system work together to provide the plant with food, water, and soil nutrients.

Plant body systems respond to the environment.

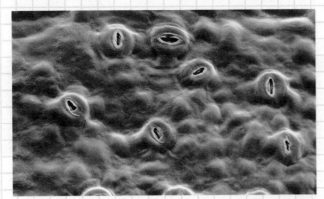

C. Describe the cause and effect relationships between conditions in the environment, such as light and a plant's response to light.

Animal Bodies as Systems

These animals are all mammals, but they have different, specialized body structures that help them survive.

By the end of this lesson . . .

you will be able to evaluate how survival needs of animals are met by systems working together.

Go online to view the digital version of the Hands-On Lab for this lesson and to download additional lab resources.

CAN YOU EXPLAIN IT?

How does this nautilus move and catch food?

The chambered nautilus can grow up to 25 cm—small enough to fit within the edges of a regular-sized sheet of paper. The chambered nautilus lives near tropical coral reefs and eats fish, shrimp, crab, and the remains of dead animals.

Fossil records show that nautiluses have been in the oceans for about 500 million years, with very little change in body structure. Like squids and octopuses, relatives of the nautilus, nautiluses have tentacles. Unlike their relatives, the nautilus has nearly 100 tentacles! Its tentacles do not have suckers but instead have ridges. Under the tentacles, a siphon can push out jets of water. The siphon is flexible, so the jets of water can be pointed in different directions. Another main feature of the nautilus is a structure that is often described as a parrot-like beak.

1. Think about another animal that has tentacles or a beak. How does that animal use these structures to move and catch food?

EVIDENCE NOTEBOOK As you explore the lesson, gather evidence to help you explain how the body systems of the nautilus function.

© Houghton Mifflin Harcourt • Image Credits: ©Wlifred Y Wong/Photographer's Choice RF/ Getty Images

Comparing Animal Body Systems

When we think of animals we often think of feathered or furry animals, but sponges, corals, and worms are animals too. Animals live on land, underground, in freshwater and in salt water—in nearly every place on Earth where there is life. Some animals even live in or on other animals!

The Animal Body

Animal bodies come in many shapes and sizes, but they have some characteristics in common. All animals are multicellular. Animals have four basic tissue types: nervous, epithelial, connective, and muscle. Nervous tissue functions as a messaging system within the body. Epithelial tissue protects and forms boundaries, and is found in organs such as skin. Connective tissue, including bones and blood, holds parts of the body together and provides support. Muscle tissue produces movement.

   The organs in an animal are made up of two or more of these tissue types. For example, the human heart is made up of muscle, nervous, and epithelial tissues. Organs are organized into systems that perform specific functions, such as digestion of food or delivery of oxygen. The types of tissues, organs, and organ systems present in an animal depend on the type of animal and its needs.

2. **Discuss** Look at the photos and read the captions to learn about the animals shown in the table. With a partner, choose two of the animals to compare and contrast in a Venn diagram.

both

Animal Diversity

Animals are classified into at least 30 groups, called *phyla*. The nine phyla in this table contain most of the animals that exist on Earth today.

This **barrel sponge** belongs to the phylum Porifera. It lives in coral reefs and other shallow ocean waters. Sponges do not have mouths. Instead, they filter food particles from the water that passes through their bodies.

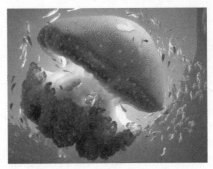

The phylum Cnidaria includes sea anemones, corals, and **jellyfish** such as the one shown here. Jellyfish bodies are made entirely of soft tissues. They have one body opening where food goes in and waste goes out.

This animal, commonly called a **flatworm,** belongs to the phylum Platyhelminthes. Platyhelminthes have a well-developed muscular system but do not have specialized circulatory, respiratory, or skeletal systems.

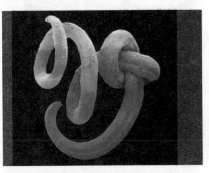

Members of the phylum Nematoda are commonly called nematodes or **roundworms.** Nematodes do not have a body system for moving nutrients and oxygen throughout the body. Instead, nutrients are distributed in their rounded body cavity.

Animals in the phylum Mollusca live on land, in freshwater, and in the ocean. Snails, slugs, squids, octopuses, and nautiluses are mollusks. This **bigfin reef squid** moves by jet propulsion—jets of water squirt through a tube-like structure called a siphon.

Animals in the phylum Annelida include this **earthworm.** Earthworms have a body filled with fluid. They move by manipulating the fluid pressure in the cavity to produce force.

Most animals of the phylum Arthropoda are insects. Spiders, scorpions, and crabs, like this **red rock crab,** are also arthropods. All arthropods have an external skeleton, called an exoskeleton.

All members of the phylum Echinodermata live in the ocean. Echinoderms include sea urchins, sand dollars, sea cucumbers, and sea stars. Echinoderms come in many shapes, but many have five-parts around a central point, like this **sea star.**

Animals in the phylum Chordata include birds, reptiles, fishes, amphibians, and mammals, such as this **okapi.** All chordates have a head, tail, spinal cord, and bilateral symmetry—the right and left sides of the body are mirror images of each other.

Functions of Animal Bodies

Animal bodies are systems that perform all the functions needed for life. Animal body systems break down food to get energy, supply cells with oxygen, and get rid of wastes. They enable animals to move, respond to their environment, and reproduce.

Digest Food and Eliminate Wastes

All animals eat other organisms to get energy and nutrients. The **digestive system** breaks down food that the body uses for energy, growth, and repair. Teeth and other specialized structures help animals break down food mechanically. Digestive enzymes in saliva and in the stomachs of animals help them break down food chemically. The digestive system also eliminates solid waste produced by the process of digestion.

Animals need to eliminate other wastes such as excess water, carbon dioxide, and toxins produced as the result of cellular processes. The **excretory system** removes wastes from the body. The skin, lungs, and kidneys are animal organs that help rid the body of waste products. For example, excess salts are released through the skin when an animal sweats. Waste products are filtered from blood as it flows through the kidneys. When you breathe out, or exhale, carbon dioxide and water vapor are released from your lungs.

Digestive System

Relationship Between Diet and Tooth Shape

The crabeater seal is an aquatic mammal that eats krill, tiny shrimp-like crustaceans. It filters the krill from the water as it swims. A tiger shark is a fierce predator that eats a wide variety of prey. Its large jaw and strong bite can penetrate the hard shell of a sea turtle.

3. Which teeth do you think belong to the crabeater seal and which belong to the tiger shark? Write the name in the box provided.

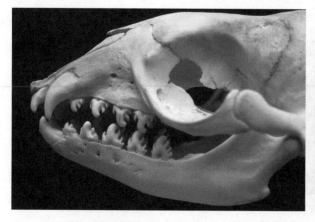

Deliver Oxygen and Nutrients

Most animals need oxygen to live. Animal cells use oxygen to release energy from food. The **respiratory system** takes in oxygen and releases carbon dioxide. Depending on the animal, oxygen enters the body through the skin, lungs, gills, or other specialized organs. The oxygen can be delivered directly to the tissues and cells of the body, or it can be sent to the circulatory system. The **circulatory system** carries oxygen, water, and nutrients to all the cells of the body. In some animals, such as mammals, the circulatory system includes two subsystems: the cardiovascular system and the lymphatic system. The cardiovascular system includes the heart and blood vessels. The heart acts as a pump to move blood through the body's blood vessels. The lymphatic system transports fluid that helps the body fight infection.

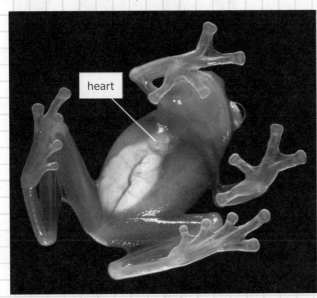

heart

The glass frog has transparent skin on its abdomen. This type of frog lives primarily in warm, humid, forested areas from southern Mexico to northern Colombia.

---

4. **Draw** Compare the frog with the diagram of the human cardiovascular system. Draw your own diagram of the frog's heart and blood vessels that you can see in the photo.

heart

Cardiovascular System

Movement and Support

All animals are able to move at some point in their life cycle. A **muscular system** is a body system that provides internal and external movement for an animal. Most animals have muscles for movement, but some animals use other body structures, such as hair-like cilia.

Muscles can attach to the skeleton to produce movement. An animal skeleton can be made of bones or other hard, nonbony structures, such as spines or crystals. A skeleton can be external, like the exoskeleton of insects. An internal skeletal system, or endoskeleton, is a framework that provides support for the body.

This blue cicada is emerging from its exoskeleton to start the next phase of its life cycle.

5. The exoskeleton of an insect provides a stiff, protective armor. Despite the protection, how might an exoskeleton be a disadvantage for growth and movement?

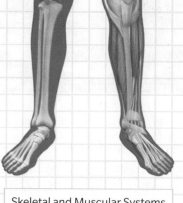

Skeletal and Muscular Systems

© Houghton Mifflin Harcourt • Image Credits: ©George Grall/National Geographic Magazines/Getty Images

Information Processing

All animals must be able to detect and react to conditions in their environments. The **nervous system** collects and processes information. The nervous system in most animals is a network of branching nerves that communicates messages between the brain and other parts of the body. In some animals, the brain is simply a cluster of nerve cells, while in others, it is complex and made up of many structures that work together.

Animals use a variety of structures to gather information from the environment. Eyes and ears are familiar organs, but animals also use hairs, skin, and antennae to collect information. Butterflies taste with their feet, and snakes smell with their tongues!

EVIDENCE NOTEBOOK

6. The nautilus does not have a skeleton but has an external shell that it can close completely. The nautilus pulls water inside a cavity in the shell, which is then expelled through the muscular siphon. Record how you think the nautilus body provides support and movement.

Analyze Structure and Function in Insect Respiration

Insects exchange gases with their environment through internal air tubes, called *tracheae*. These tubes branch to all parts of the insect's body, delivering oxygen directly to the tissues. The tracheae connect to the outside air through paired holes in the insect's body segments, called *spiracles*. Muscular valves control the opening and closing of the spiracles. Active insects that require more oxygen can use pumping motions of their abdomens to force more air into and out of the spiracles.

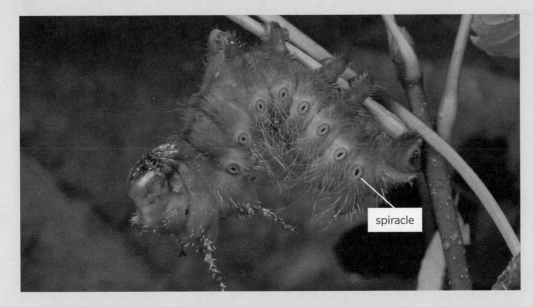

spiracle

The spiracles of this imperial moth caterpillar are visible as round openings along the body segments.

7. The circulatory system of an insect transports water, nutrients, and wastes, but does not transport oxygen. Why not?

   A. The tracheae connect to the circulatory system in the insect body.

   B. The insect body absorbs oxygen from nutrients and water.

   C. The tracheae deliver oxygen directly to all the tissues in the insect's body.

8. Spiracles can be covered with hairs or spines. How might this structure relate to its function?

   _____

   _____

   _____

   _____

   _____

Analyzing Animal Body System Interactions

Animal Body Systems Interact to Perform Functions

Animals need to find and eat food, they need to move, and they need to respond to their environment. They may also need to maintain stable internal conditions, such as temperature. Individual body systems perform these functions, but not in isolation. Almost everything an animal needs to remain healthy requires its body systems to work together. For example, many systems work together with the digestive system to provide nutrients for cells. The nervous system sends signals to muscles in the digestive organs to contract and relax to help break up food and move it through the digestive system. Blood then carries the digested food particles from the digestive system to all the cells in the body.

The parrot fish lives on and near coral reefs. These fish got their common name from a jaw structure that looks like a parrot beak. The fish use the hard structures that make up the beak to scrape algae from coral reefs.

9. Which body systems do you think are working together at each stage of the digestive process described below? Enter the systems in the table below.

Process	Systems
chewing of food	
movement of food through the body	
absorption and transport of nutrients	
getting rid of carbon dioxide	

 EVIDENCE NOTEBOOK

10. The nautilus has ridged tentacles and a powerful parrot-like beak. It has poor vision and hunts mostly at night. Describe how you think the nautilus body structures help it catch and eat food. What sensory stimulus do you think it uses?

Whale Breaching Behavior

Whales are aquatic mammals that display a behavior called *breaching*. Breaching involves jumping out of the water, whirling around, and landing with a loud splash.

1. The whale detects a stimulus in the environment that begins the breech response.

2. The heart pumps faster as the whale swims rapidly to gain momentum.

3. The whale raises its entire body above the surface of the water.

 Explore ONLINE!

Language SmArts
Sequence an Animal Response

Scientists have several ideas about why these animals perform this behavior. They may be communicating a change of route to other whales in the pod, claiming territory, attracting a mate, removing body parasites, or simply having fun!

11. Choose one of the ideas about why whales breach. Write a detailed sequence of events describing the interaction of body systems that happens when the whale breaches.

Responding to the Environment

12. The sensory organs in an animal's nervous system detect changes in the environment. These changes are communicated to other body systems so that they can work to respond. Complete the table to explain how systems work together in each example.

A cricket scurries across the sand in the Sahara where the fennec fox lives.

Mosquitoes are flying in the air above a marsh where a dragonfly is perched on a milkweed.

| Detection:
The motion of the cricket is detected by the ears of the fox. | Detection: |
| Response: | Response:
The dragonfly flies off the milkweed to chase and capture a meal. |

13. Name something you react to in your environment. How do you detect it? How do your body systems work together to respond?

Hands-On Lab
Measure System Response to Exercise

You will perform an exercise and measure the responses of your respiratory and cardiovascular systems.

When you exercise, your body systems work together to respond to changing needs for oxygen in your cells. Animals need more oxygen when they chase prey, run from predators, and travel long distances.

Procedure

STEP 1 Make a plan for how you will measure your breathing rate (*b*) and pulse (*p*) before you exercise. Decide how long you will rest before collecting the data.

STEP 2 Measure your before-exercise breathing rate and pulse. Record the data in the table below.

STEP 3 Make a plan for how you will measure your breathing rate and pulse after you exercise. Think about what type of exercise you will do and for how long.

STEP 4 Follow your plan to exercise. Measure your after-exercise breathing rate and pulse. Record the data for 3 trials in the table below.

STEP 5 Repeat the procedure two more times.

	Before Exercise		After Exercise	
	breathing rate	pulse	breathing rate	pulse
Trial 1				
Trial 2				
Trial 3				
Average				

Analysis and Conclusions

STEP 6 **Do the Math** For each column in your table, calculate the average of the three trials. Are the values recorded for each trial the same?

STEP 7 How did the change in pulse compare to the change in breathing rate? Did one change more than the other?

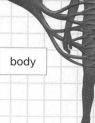

lungs

heart

body

STEP 8 Look at the diagram that shows the connection between the circulatory and the respiratory systems. Use the diagram and your data to explain why pulse and breathing rates change when you exercise.

This diagram shows the path that blood takes through the human heart and lungs. Blood is pumped from the right side of the heart to the lungs. From the lungs it returns to the left side of the heart. The blood is then pumped from the left side of the heart to the body. It flows to the tiny capillaries around every part of the body before returning to the right side of the heart.

Engineer It
Predict Effects of System Failure

Animal body systems rely on other systems and subsystems to perform functions. The failure of any system or subsystem may have predicable results. Consider the following scenario: A leopard cub fell out of a tree while learning to climb. He suffered a collapsed lung. A collapsed lung does not function to move air in and out of the body. How does the collapsed lung affect the leopard cub's other body systems?

14. Collaborate On a separate sheet of paper, produce a diagram to explain how the damaged lung affects other systems. Identify inputs and outputs of the respiratory system in your response.

Continue Your Exploration

Name: _____ **Date:** _____

Check out the path below or go online to choose one of the other paths shown.

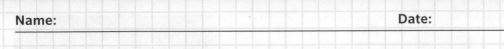

| Careers in Science | • Hands-On Labs 👋
 • Leonardo da Vinci
 • Propose Your Own Path | *Go online to choose one of these other paths.* |

Animal Scientists

Zoology is the study of all aspects of animals, including animal behavior, evolution, classification, structures and functions, interactions with ecosystems, interactions with humans, and many other topics. Within these topics, animals may be studied at different scales. For example, scientists study animals at a genetic level and a cellular level. They also study animals at an organismal level.

Entomology

An entomologist studies insects, such as the Eucharitid wasp shown here. Since most animals on Earth are insects, entomologists may study a very broad range of species and topics. Research topics include tracking insect reproduction and migration. Other areas of research apply to pollination, agriculture, forensics, and human disease.

1. If you were to study a group of animals, which group do you think you would be most interested in? Explain why.

© Houghton Mifflin Harcourt • Image Credits: (r) ©Rundstedt B. Rovillos/Moment/Getty Images

Continue Your Exploration

Herpetology

A herpetologist studies amphibians, like the frog shown here, and reptiles. Some herpetologists work at a college or university and conduct research. Others work with a wildlife agency or a museum. One of many interesting herpetology research topics relates to the North American wood frog that can freeze solid in the winter and continue living after thawing in the spring. The ability to freeze and thaw living tissue could be applied in medical fields—for example, to help extend the time that organs can be stored for transplant.

Ornithology

An ornithologist studies birds, like the hawk shown in the picture. Ornithologists may work to learn more about a particular species in order to support conservation of the species and its habitat. This is a field of study where amateur bird watchers make a significant contribution. They help professional ornithologists by providing data about bird species in their area.

2. Physiology is the study of how living systems function. How do you think zoology contributes to the understanding of human physiology?

3. If you were a herpetologist studying turtle migration, what questions would you ask to help you understand how and why the turtles migrate?

4. **Collaborate** Work with a partner to learn more about research in a field of zoology. You can also research a different branch of zoology. For example, mammalogists study mammals, such as wolves, cats, and rodents. Primatologists focus on monkeys and apes. Malacologists study mollusks, such as the nautilus you were introduced to in the beginning of the lesson. Ichthyologists study fish and other marine life. Gather relevant information from print and digital sources. Using your own words, summarize some of the research topics that you learn about. Remember to cite your sources.

Can You Explain It?

Name: _____   **Date:** _____

Think back to the chambered nautilus and its tentacles, siphon, and beak.

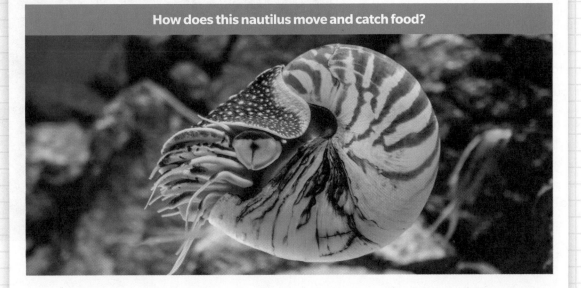

How does this nautilus move and catch food?

 EVIDENCE NOTEBOOK

Refer to the notes in your Evidence Notebook to help you construct an explanation for how the nautilus's body systems work together.

1. State your claim. Make sure your claim fully explains how the nautilus's body structures meet the needs of the animal.

2. Summarize the evidence you have gathered to support your claim and explain your reasoning.

Checkpoints

Answer the following questions to check your understanding of the lesson.

Use the photo below to answer Questions 3 and 4.

3. Which two systems are represented in this model?

   A. circulatory and respiratory

   B. nervous and circulatory

   C. excretory and respiratory

   D. nervous and digestive

4. Blood travels through the circulatory / excretory system to the lungs / kidneys where it interacts with the digestive / respiratory system to exchange gases.

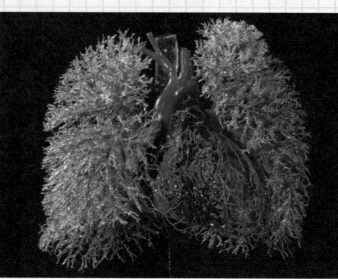

The blood vessels, heart, and lungs were filled with a plastic polymer to make this cast.

Use the photo below to answer Questions 5 and 6.

5. Which stimulus is the cheetah responding to? Circle all that apply.

   A. The cheetah is responding to the motion of the wildebeest.

   B. The cheetah is responding to hunger felt inside its digestive system.

   C. The cheetah is responding to its internal temperature.

6. These animals' bodies are complex systems composed of many interacting subsystems. The excretory / digestive / muscular system is moving the animals' bodies.

   Running at top speeds, the wildebeest and cheetah are using their digestive / muscular / nervous systems to take in information from their surroundings and communicate these signals to the body.

   The animals' circulatory / digestive / muscular systems are working to deliver oxygen-rich blood to cells in all parts of their bodies. Their circulatory / digestive / respiratory systems are taking oxygen into their bodies and working to get rid of carbon dioxide.

Interactive Review

Complete this section to review the main concepts of the lesson.

Animal bodies are systems that perform all the functions needed by an animal to survive.

A. Describe the basic functions of animal body systems.

Animal body systems work together to meet the survival needs of the animal.

B. Use a specific example to explain how the interactions of two or more body systems work together to perform a function.

Information Processing in Animals

Ameiva lizards can communicate with each other using chemical signals that are detected by their sensory systems.

By the end of this lesson . . .

you will be able to explain the relationship between information processing and animal behavior.

Go online to view the digital version of the Hands-On Lab for this lesson and to download additional lab resources.

CAN YOU EXPLAIN IT?

Why is it so difficult to catch a fly?

Houseflies can be found anywhere there are animals. They feed on garbage, manure, or softened food, like this biscuit left on the counter.

1. Have you ever tried to swat a fly? If so, you know that it isn't easy. How do you think the fly is able to anticipate your moves and avoid your swatter?

EVIDENCE NOTEBOOK As you explore the lesson, gather evidence to help you explain how a fly processes information.

Describing Information Processing in Animals

Think about what your body is doing right now. What can you see? feel? smell? hear? Without even thinking about it, your body is sensing all kinds of information from the environment. Animal bodies constantly receive and process information from the environment. When an animal body receives information, it processes the information and then responds to it.

In order to survive, an animal might need to respond to danger, the need for food and water, or changes in temperature. These responses help an animal maintain homeostasis. When internal and external environments change, **homeostasis** is the process by which the inside of the body maintains stable conditions.

Animal Responses to Changes in Temperature

2. Think of some behaviors an animal might perform to cool down or warm up. Record the behaviors in the correct box of the feedback diagram.

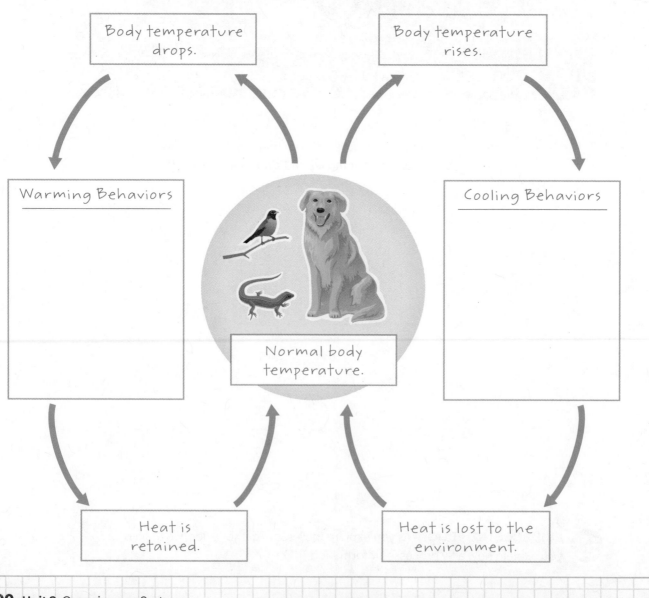

Body temperature drops.

Body temperature rises.

Warming Behaviors

Cooling Behaviors

Normal body temperature.

Heat is retained.

Heat is lost to the environment.

Engineer It
Analyze System Feedback

Homeostasis is controlled through feedback. *Feedback* is a cycle of events in which information from one step controls or affects a previous step. Feedback can be positive or negative. Negative feedback occurs when the body senses a change in its internal environment and activates processes that will slow or prevent the change. Positive feedback occurs when the body activates processes that increase or reinforce the change.

3. A dog responds to the stimulus of feeling hot by panting. When the dog cools down, the dog will stop panting. The control of the dog's body temperature is an example of *negative / positive* feedback.

To help cool off, this dog is panting. Water evaporates from the dog's mouth, resulting in heat loss.

Sensing and Transmitting Information

Specialized cells in an animal's nervous system are called sensory receptors. **Sensory receptors** help an animal gather information about its environment. Sensory receptors are especially plentiful in sensory organs—the skin, ears, nose, mouth, and eyes—but they also occur in other parts of the body. Different types of sensory receptors respond to different environmental messages, such as light, heat, or pressure. This type of environmental message is called a *stimulus.* For example, a sensory receptor could detect pressure from a butterfly landing on your finger. When a sensory receptor detects a stimulus, it sends the information to the brain in the form of electrical energy. The information travels through specialized cells called *neurons.* One group of neurons carries information from sensory receptors to the brain. Another group of neurons carries information from the brain to various parts of the body, telling them how to respond.

Sensory receptor

Neuron

Path of sensory information

4. Read the descriptions about each animal below. Which stimulus might each of these animals be responding to? You may use more than one stimulus.

light	odor
motion	sound

	Turkey vultures are scavengers. They do not hunt their own food; they eat animals that are already dead.	type of stimulus:
	This spider is wrapping up prey that got caught in its web.	type of stimulus:
	Bats use echolocation to find prey in the dark. The bat emits a noise that bounces off of objects, allowing the bat to estimate the location of the object.	type of stimulus:

Types of Sensory Receptors

Sensory receptors can be organized by the kind of stimuli they detect and respond to. *Mechanical receptors* detect pressure, movement, and tension. For example, fish have a specialized sense organ that detects vibrations in the water, helping them to navigate and hunt. Mechanical receptors also detect the motion of sound waves, allowing animals to hear.

Chemical receptors detect chemical signals, such as odors and tastes. Some animals have chemical receptors in their nose and mouth, but others have chemical receptors on their antennae or limbs.

Electromagnetic receptors detect electromagnetic radiation, such as light. Different kinds of animals have different electromagnetic receptors, so each kind of animal can see specific parts of the electromagnetic spectrum. Your eyes detect visible light, but some other animals can detect infrared radiation or ultraviolet light.

5. Discuss With a partner, discuss the types of receptors being used by the animals in the photos in the table.

Processing Sensory Information

Most animals have a brain that organizes and processes information from sensory receptors. Animal brains can be just a cluster of neurons, or they can be made up of many structures that work together. Different animals process information at different rates. For example, scientific evidence suggests that smaller animals may process visual information faster than larger animals.

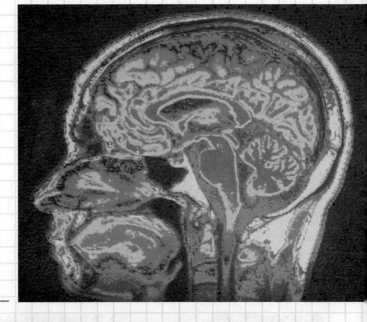

This is a magnetic resonance imaging (MRI) of a human head.

Major Areas of the Human Cerebral Cortex

The cerebral cortex is an important part of the human brain. Explore the image to find out how information is processed in the major areas of the cerebral cortex.

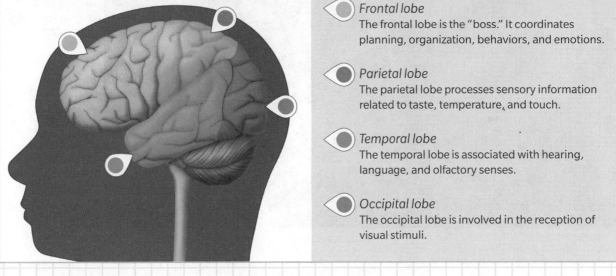

Frontal lobe
The frontal lobe is the "boss." It coordinates planning, organization, behaviors, and emotions.

Parietal lobe
The parietal lobe processes sensory information related to taste, temperature, and touch.

Temporal lobe
The temporal lobe is associated with hearing, language, and olfactory senses.

Occipital lobe
The occipital lobe is involved in the reception of visual stimuli.

6. How might damage to the temporal lobe of the brain affect a person? Which sensory receptor messages would be affected?

7. Think back to the picture of the fly at the beginning of the lesson. What types of stimuli is the fly responding to when you try to catch it? Which body structures might be involved? Record your evidence.

Language SmArts
Explain Sensory Receptor Patterns

Not all parts of your body are as sensitive to touch as others. Your fingers, for example, have many sensory receptors, so they are very sensitive to touch. Other body parts—your back and your calf, for example—have fewer sensory receptors and are much less sensitive to touch.

Fingers are very sensitive to touch because they have so many mechanical receptors as well as other types of sensory receptors.

8. Why do you think the parts of the body have such differences? Write an argument to explain the differences in the sensitivities of the different parts of the body.

_____

_____

_____

_____

_____

_____

_____

_____

_____

_____

© Houghton Mifflin Harcourt • Image Credits: ©Herbie Springer/Alamy Images

Describing Animal Responses to Information

When the brain receives sensory messages, it determines what to do with the information. Sensory inputs can result in an immediate response, and they can also be stored in the brain for use in the future. For example, an animal might perform the immediate behavior of spitting out a bad-tasting prey. The animal might also store that information as memory and avoid the prey when they meet again.

9. Look at the lion and the porcupines. What immediate behaviors might each animal perform? What might be stored as memory for each animal? Record your answers.

	behavior	memory
lion		
porcupines		

Behavior

The set of actions taken by an organism in response to stimuli is called **behavior**. Animals perform behaviors to survive. Some animal behaviors do not require learning or experience. For example, newborn whales know how to swim as soon as they are born. Behaviors that do not require learning or experience are called *innate* behaviors. Animals are born knowing these behaviors, but they are triggered by things that happen in the animal's environment.

Other behaviors develop through memories and experience, and from observing the actions of other animals. These behaviors that depend on memory are *learned* behaviors. For example, some birds learn their songs by listening to other individuals. Young animals can learn to hunt and even use tools by watching adults.

Do the Math
Analyze Hibernation

Hibernation is a period of inactivity that some animals experience in winter. Animals that hibernate are able to conserve energy during the months when food may be scarce. Many animals increase their food intake in the months before hibernation. The extra body fat they gain will help them survive during the months they will spend without eating. The graph below shows how two variables—weight gain and month of the year—relate.

The hazel dormouse is a tiny rodent that hibernates for about half the year, from fall to spring.

10. Which variable is the independent variable? Which variable is the dependent variable? Explain how you know which variable is independent and which is dependent.

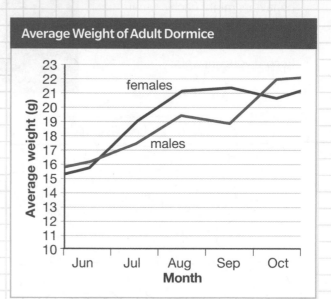

Average Weight of Adult Dormice

(graph: x-axis "Month" from Jun to Oct; y-axis "Average weight (g)" from 10 to 23; two lines labeled "females" and "males")

11. During which time period do both the males and females gain weight most rapidly?

12. What other factors besides a change in feeding behavior may be affecting weight gain by the dormice during the summer months?

Memory

Information can be stored in the brain as **memory**. Information that gets stored as memory can be an event, such as an encounter with predator or prey. Animals can also remember information related to sensory stimuli. Odor memory can help animals identify their infants or family members. Visual memory can help them remember locations of food sources or migration routes. Memory allows an animal to respond to its environment more efficiently. For example, an animal that can remember the location of a food source will spend less time searching for food and more time eating!

Hands-On Lab
Measure Reaction Time

Behaviors are the result of systems working together. To catch an object, your brain sends a message to the muscles in your arm. The time it takes for the message to travel from your brain to your arm is called your reaction time. You will measure your reaction to a falling object.

MATERIALS
• chair
• meterstick

Procedure and Analysis

STEP 1 One person should sit in a chair with one arm in a "handshake" position. The other person should stand facing the person in the chair, holding the meterstick vertically so that the lower end is between the sitting person's thumb and forefinger. Observe where on the meterstick's scale the sitting person's thumb and forefinger are. Record the data in the table.

STEP 2 Make sure the sitting student has the thumb and forefinger far enough apart for the meterstick to fall through. The person holding the meterstick should drop it without warning. The person sitting should catch the meterstick as quickly as possible. Record the location of the sitting person's thumb and forefinger on the meterstick's scale after catching the meterstick.

STEP 3 Determine the distance the meterstick fell and record the data in the table.

STEP 4 Repeat Steps 1–3 two more times.

STEP 5 Calculate the average distance the meterstick fell in the three trials.

	Finger position before drop (cm)	Finger position when caught (cm)	Distance meterstick fell (cm)
Trial 1			
Trial 2			
Trial 3			

Average distance meterstick fell: _____

STEP 6 Describe the flow of information from sensory receptors to behavioral response. Make note of all the body systems that are involved in the response you tested in this activity.

STEP 7 Identify the cause and the effect in this activity.

STEP 8 Compare your group's data with the data of another group. How did the data compare? What factors might explain any differences in reaction times?

STEP 9 **Discuss** In the activity, your reaction time probably got faster each time you caught the meterstick. With a partner, discuss how memory and experience contribute to a faster reaction time.

EVIDENCE NOTEBOOK

13. Look back at the photo of the fly. Does the fly have a fast reaction to your swatter or a slow reaction? What advantage might the fly have that you do not?

Engineer It

Compare Information Processing in Different Systems

A computer is used to gather, organize, and store information through a series of events that is similar to the way an animal brain processes information. Use what you've learned about how the animal body processes inputs from the environment to think about how a computer processes information.

14. Order the sequence of events by placing the number next to the step.

_____ CPU sends signal to screen

_____ Letter "A" appears on screen

_____ Central processing unit (CPU) processes data

_____ Someone taps the "A" key on a keyboard

_____ Information travels from the keyboard to processing system

15. What is the main similarity between information processing in an animal and information processing in a computer?

_____

_____

_____

_____

_____

_____

Continue Your Exploration

Name: _____   Date: _____

Check out the path below or go online to choose one of the other paths shown.

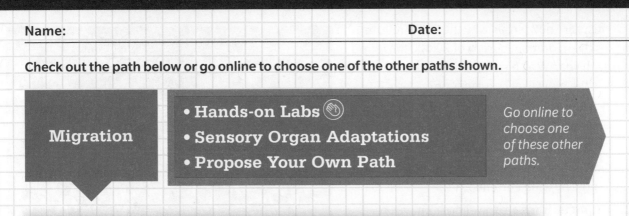

| Migration | • **Hands-on Labs** 🖐
• **Sensory Organ Adaptations**
• **Propose Your Own Path** | *Go online to choose one of these other paths.* |

Animals travel long distances in response to seasonal weather changes and changes in the availability of food. This type of travel is called *migration*. Migration is a seasonal movement from one place to another. Birds, mammals, reptiles, fish, and even insects migrate. Migration is often related to food or reproductive needs.

Monarch butterflies travel from the United States to Mexico to avoid the cold winter temperatures.

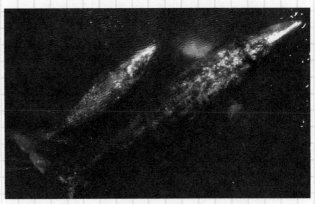

This gray whale and her calf are migrating north from California to summer feeding grounds in the Arctic.

1. If migration is thought of in terms of cause and effect, migration can be considered the effect. What is the cause of the monarch migration? What is the cause of the gray whale migration?

Continue Your Exploration

2. Scientists are not certain why the little Arctic tern makes the migration journey of 70,000 km round trip each year. Which statement below do you think is the most likely explanation?

A. The Arctic terns are following patterns of food availability and favorable wind conditions from pole to pole.

B. The Arctic terns are being carried from pole to pole by wind currents.

C. The Arctic terns are traveling from pole to pole to find mates.

The Arctic tern makes the longest known annual migration—from the South Pole to the North Pole and back again.

3. Current research suggests that olfactory memory may play a role in the migration of salmon, as well as some other animals. What type of sensory receptors do you think the salmon are using to navigate their migration path? Explain your answer.

Salmon are hatched in freshwater and then migrate to the ocean. When salmon are ready to reproduce, they migrate back to the freshwater areas where they were hatched.

4. Collaborate Research a migration pattern of one of the animals from the previous page or another animal of your choice. Collaborate to make a visual summary or map of the pattern of migration.

Can You Explain It?

Name: _____ **Date:** _____

Think back to that pesky fly at the beginning of the lesson.

Why is it so difficult to catch a fly?

 EVIDENCE NOTEBOOK

Refer to the notes in your Evidence Notebook to help you construct an explanation for how this fly avoids your swatter.

1. State your claim. Make sure your claim fully explains how the fly processes information from the environment.

2. Summarize the evidence you have gathered to support your claim and explain your reasoning.

Checkpoints

Answer the following questions to check your understanding of the lesson.

Use the image to answer questions 3–4.

3. Butterflies have membranes on different parts of their bodies that vibrate in response to waves in the air. What type of sensory input are these membranes transmitting? Circle your answer.

   A. light

   B. sound

   C. odor

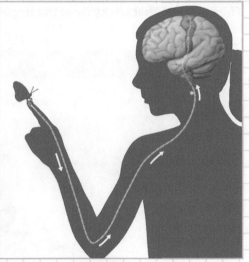

4. The person in the image is detecting the butterfly using _____ and _____ receptors.

Use the image to answer questions 5–6.

5. Place the sequence of events in the correct order by numbering.

   _____ Sensory information about change in season is sent to brain.

   _____ Brain signals the animal to respond by storing food for winter.

   _____ Brain stores the information as a memory.

   _____ Sensory information about stored food location is sent to brain.

   _____ Nervous system perceives a change in season.

   _____ Brain processes sensory information about season change.

This red squirrel is burying food. Squirrels store food in many locations in preparation for winter. The squirrel will return to some of these locations during the winter to uncover and eat the stored food.

6. The route taken to a stored food source is the result of *immediate behavior / stored memory* by the squirrel. A hawk flying overhead as the squirrel travels to the food will result in an *immediate behavior / stored memory* by the squirrel.

Interactive Review

Complete this section to review the main concepts of the lesson.

Animal bodies gather and process information from their environment.

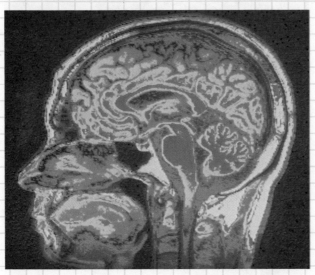

A. Draw a picture or flow chart to show how an animal body processes information from the environment.

Animals have sensory receptors that respond to stimuli and send messages to the brain.

B. What is the relationship between memory and behavior?

Choose one of the activities to explore how this unit connects to other topics.

Physical Science Connection

Using Imaging Technology Today, scientists and doctors can use magnetic resonance imaging (MRI) or computed tomography (CT) scans when they want to assess the health of and study the interactions among an organism's organs, tissues, and other internal structures. MRIs use a magnetic field and radio waves, and CT scans use x-rays.

Research and write an informative essay on how either MRIs or CT scans work. What recent developments have been discovered about humans' internal structures through the use of these technologies?

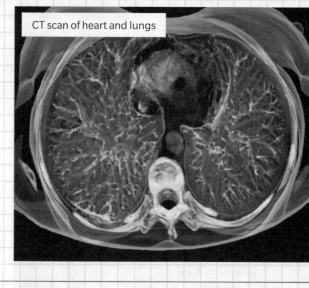
CT scan of heart and lungs

Health Connection

Physical Therapy and Body System Function
When people are injured, they sometimes undergo physical therapy to heal their injuries. Using tests, exercises, and equipment, physical therapists work with a patient's skeletal, muscular, and nervous system to restore movement.

Research the career of a physical therapist. Discover the techniques physical therapists use to rehabilitate torn, sprained, or strained muscles and other injuries. If possible, interview a local physical therapist about his or her job. Present your findings to your class.

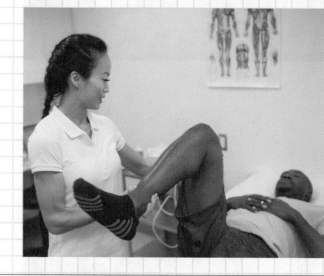

Art Connection

The Golden Ratio and the Fibonacci Sequence
Many plants have structures that conform to the Golden Ratio, which is approximately equal to 1.618. The Golden Ratio is related to a series of numbers called the Fibonacci sequence. Both have inspired artists and architects.

Research the Golden Ratio, the Fibonacci sequence, and how the two are related. Then research paintings, sculptures, or buildings that incorporate the two. Choose several works of art or buildings and present them to the class, explaining how they incorporate the Golden Ratio and the Fibonacci sequence.

The Great Wave by Katsushika Hokusai

Name: _____   Date: _____

Use the diagram of the snake to answer Questions 1–2.

1. The diagram shows the snake's skeletal system. Which other body system works with the skeletal system to help provide movement?

   A. Digestive system

   B. Muscular system

   C. Excretory system

   D. Respiratory System

2. The snake's skin performs specialized functions for the body, including protection from injury and disease. The skin is made up of several tissue types. Therefore, the snake's skin is an example of a(n)

   A. tissue.

   B. organ.

   C. organ system.

   D. body structure.

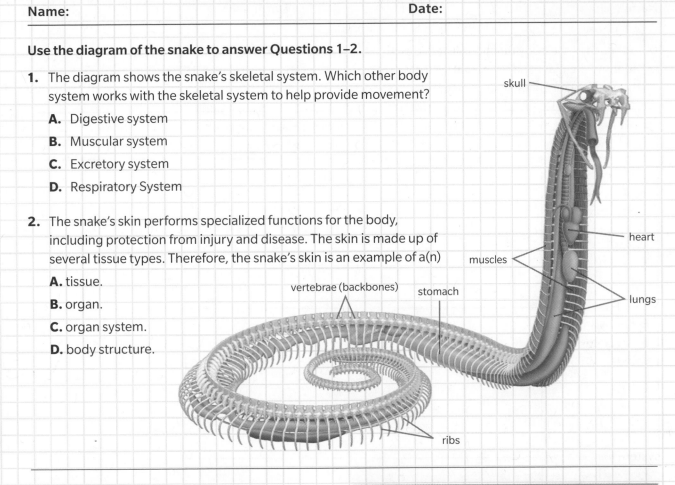

skull

heart

muscles

lungs

vertebrae (backbones)

stomach

ribs

Use the diagram to answer Questions 3–4.

3. An animal's skeletal system performs the function of food production / support / transport, just as the root / shoot system of the sunflower does for that plant.

4. Which of these plant body functions requires interaction between the root and shoot system?

   A. getting water to all parts of the plant

   B. anchoring the plant to the ground

   C. collecting energy from sunlight

   D. moving nutrients throughout the plant

5. The Venus flytrap is a plant that has hairs on its leaves, which sense movement. These hairs are an example of chemical / electromagnetic / mechanical sensory receptors.

stem

leaves

roots

© Houghton Mifflin Harcourt

Name: _____   **Date:** _____

6. For each of the body functions listed, describe the function in terms of cause and effect. Identify the plant and/or animal systems involved, and describe any related patterns between plant and animal bodies.

Body Functions	Systems	Cause-and-Effect Relationships	Patterns in Plants and Animal Bodies
Moving water and nutrients throughout body			
Getting energy from food			
Providing support for the body			
Regulating oxygen and carbon dioxide			
Responding to the environment			

Use the illustration of the frog to answer questions 7–11.

7. Identify the environmental stimulus that the frog is perceiving.

8. Explain how both electromagnetic receptors and mechanical receptors might be involved in sensing this stimulus. Use evidence to explain your reasoning.

9. How do the sensory receptors transmit information about the stimulus to the frog's brain?

10. Describe the frog's possible responses to the information the sensory receptors have transmitted to the brain. Include a description of how the brain will cause the frog's body to act.

11. Is the frog's response to the stimuli an example of learned or innate behavior? Use evidence to explain your reasoning.

© Houghton Mifflin Harcourt

Use the diagram of a tree to answer questions 12–15.

12. Explain the levels of organization in this tree, from cells to the entire organism. Use specific examples from the diagram in your explanation.

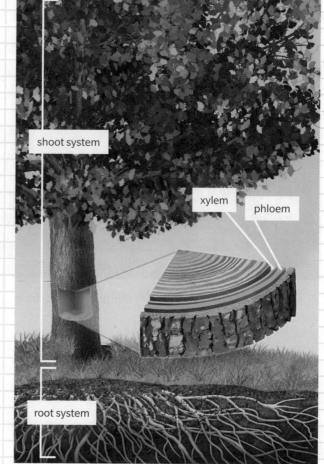

shoot system

xylem

phloem

root system

13. Leaves are plant organs. How is the health of the tree dependent on the functioning of the tree's leaves?

14. How do the tree's leaves work with other organs and organ systems to meet the basic needs of the tree?

15. At certain times, the stomata on the tree's leaves close. What environmental stimulus might cause this response? Use evidence to explain the tree's response.

Name: _____   Date: _____

How can dehydration be prevented?

Your school district wants to find the best ways to keep student athletes from becoming dehydrated during after-school practices. Your team has been assembled to help school officials, coaches, and parent volunteers devise a plan for keeping student athletes hydrated, using the diagram below, which shows some of the body systems involved in maintaining water balance in the body.

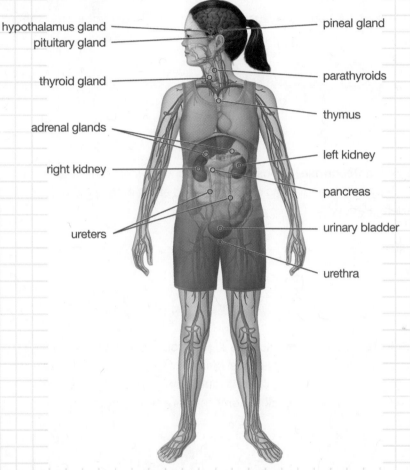

hypothalamus gland
pituitary gland
pineal gland
thyroid gland
parathyroids
thymus
adrenal glands
left kidney
right kidney
pancreas
ureters
urinary bladder
urethra

The steps below will help guide your research and develop your recommendation.

Engineer It

1. **Define the Problem** Investigate the importance of water in human body systems. Define the problem your team is trying to solve.

Engineer It

2. **Plan an Investigation** Investigate the body systems involved in maintaining water balance in the body.

3. **Conduct Research** Research the causes and symptoms of dehydration in the human body.

4. **Analyze a System Response** Choose one of the body systems that shows symptoms of dehydration and analyze the cause and effect of the system's response to dehydration.

5. **Propose a Solution** Brainstorm solutions to the problem of how to keep student athletes hydrated during practices. Make a recommendation based on your research. Explain how the solution would work with the body system you identified to bring the body back to homeostasis after dehydration.

✓ **Self-Check**

	I defined the problem of preventing dehydration in student athletes and investigated the importance of water to human body systems.
	I investigated the body systems involved in maintaining water balance in the body.
	I researched the causes and symptoms of dehydration.
	I analyzed the causes and effects of a body system's response to dehydration.
	I recommended a solution to the problem of preventing dehydration in student athletes and explained how the solution would work with the body system to bring the body back to homeostasis.

Reproduction, Heredity, and Growth

This plumage display of a male bird of paradise attracts the female. With all their needs met by the rich abundance of the tropical rain forest, birds of paradise can spend substantial time and energy on reproduction.

Bald eagles, bacteria, buttercups, and bats—these species have different traits, populate different habitats, and use different strategies to grow and reproduce. Yet all of them find ways to maximize their numbers despite limiting factors in their environment. In this unit, you will investigate how traits are passed down from parents to offspring, and explain how different factors affect the growth and successful reproduction of organisms.

Why It Matters

Here are some questions to consider as you work through the unit. Can you answer any of the questions now? Revisit these questions at the end of the unit to apply what you discover.

Questions	Notes
All life is comprised of the same basic unit, the cell. So, what is responsible for the vast diversity of life on Earth?	
What characteristics do you share with your family members? What makes you unique?	
Why would farmers, doctors, dog breeders, and engineers all care about factors that affect the traits and growth of living things?	
Why is it important to understand the different ways that living things reproduce?	
How does understanding the science behind reproduction, heredity, and growth help people make important decisions about their health, as well as the health of Earth?	

Unit Starter: Identifying Factors Related to Reproduction

Ecologists study relationships between environmental factors and reproductive success by gathering and analyzing data. This graph shows the average number of eggs laid, called clutch size, for titmouse birds during years with different amounts of caterpillars available to eat.

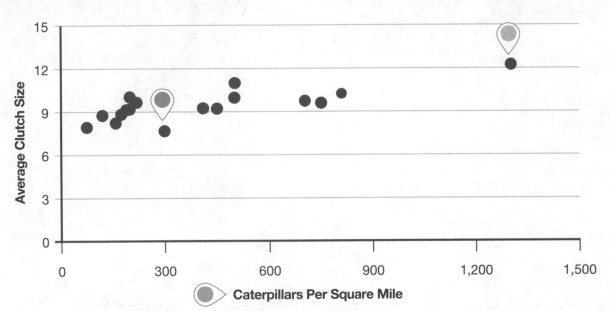

Source: Pianka, Eric R. *Evolutionary Ecology – 7th Edition – eBook.* © 2011

 The number of caterpillars available to titmouse birds in the English countryside changes from year to year due to changes in average rainfall, as well as the presence of other species that compete for food.

An unexpected environmental factor, such as a drought or fire, can reduce caterpillar populations. Birds struggling to find food must use more energy to find food, leaving less energy to produce eggs.

An abundance of caterpillars can result from higher than average rainfall or a low number of competitors. With a larger food supply, birds may lay more eggs, but the eggs may be smaller.

1. The number of caterpillars per square mile *does / does not* affect the reproductive success of titmouse birds. When there are more caterpillars available for the birds to eat, the average clutch size is *larger / smaller.*

Go online to download the Unit Project Worksheet to help you plan your project.

Unit Project

Plant Perfect

Farmer's market vendors hope to catch your eye with juicy fruits, crunchy vegetables, and vibrant flowers. Use what you know about inheritance and factors influencing plant reproduction and growth to harvest a radish crop fit for market!

Inheritance

These African cichlid fish all have a black stripe over their eyes. Do you think they could be related?

By the end of this lesson . . .

you will be able to determine how inheritance influences an organism's traits, such as fur color.

Go online to view the digital version of the Hands-On Lab for this lesson and to download additional lab resources.

CAN YOU EXPLAIN IT?

How did these kittens get their fur colors?

These kittens are all related because they have the same two parents. However, when you look at the fur colors of the kittens, you'll notice that they are not all the same.

1. Knowing the kittens' fur color, what would you predict the parents' fur looks like?

2. What explanation can you suggest for individuals of a certain type of organism being so similar to one another—and so different from one another too? Could there be some kind of information that is passed from parent to offspring?

EVIDENCE NOTEBOOK As you explore the lesson, gather evidence to help explain how the kittens got their fur color.

Investigating How Traits Are Passed from Parent to Offspring

More than 150 years ago, an Austrian monk named Gregor Mendel observed that pea plants in his garden had different forms of certain characteristics. Mendel studied the characteristics of pea plants such as seed color and flower color. Each characteristic that Mendel studied had two different forms. For example, the color of a pea could be green or yellow. These different forms are called **traits.**

Mendel noticed that when the plants reproduced, the next generations of plants did not always share the same traits of the parents. He planned an experiment to investigate how the traits of the parent plants passed on to the offspring.

3. Discuss What are some differences you notice in these pea plants?

Mendel used pea plants to study how traits are passed from parent to offspring.

Mendel's Pea Plant Investigation

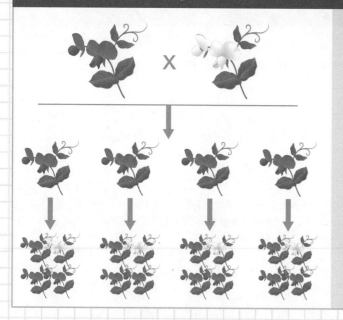

These two plants represent the parent generation. Usually, these pea plants self-pollinate. But instead, Mendel fertilized one parent plant with the pollen from the other parent plant.

These four plants represent the first generation of offspring (F1). In the F1 generation, all of the plants had purple flowers.

These plants represent the second generation of offspring (F2). Most of the F2 generation offspring have purple flowers, but some offspring have white flowers.

4. How does the presence of white flowers change from the parent generation, to first generation of offspring, to the second generation of offspring?

Mendel's Investigation Methods

Mendel studied each pea plant trait separately, always starting with plants that were true breeding for that trait. A true-breeding plant is one that will always produce offspring with a certain trait when allowed to self-pollinate. The white-flowered and purple-flowered parent plants that Mendel studied were true-breeding plants for the flower color trait. Usually pea plants self-pollinate, but Mendel *crossed* the two parent plants, meaning he fertilized one parent plant with pollen from the other parent plant. Then he let the first generation self-pollinate. He used these same methods to study other pea plant traits.

Before Mendel became a monk, he attended a university and studied science and mathematics.

Dominant and Recessive Traits

When Mendel crossed the purple-flowered and white-flowered plants, all first-generation plants had purple flowers. Mendel called this trait the *dominant trait*. Because the white flowered trait seemed to recede, or fade away, he called it the *recessive trait*. For all traits that Mendel studied, a similar pattern occurred. One of the parents' traits would not show up in the first generation. These were all recessive traits. The other trait—that shows up in all first generation offspring—was the dominant trait.

But what about the second generation of offspring? About one-fourth of these plants had white flowers—the recessive trait. The rest had purple flowers. The trait that seemed to disappear in the first generation reappeared in the second generation. Again, for all of the traits that Mendel studied, this same pattern occurred.

Language SmArts
Construct an Explanation of Trait Inheritance

What could explain the mysterious disappearance and reappearance of the recessive traits? Mendel hypothesized that each plant must have two inherited "factors" for each trait, one from each parent. Some traits, such as white flower color, only occurred if a plant received two factors for white flower color. A plant with one white flower factor and one purple flower factor would have the dominant trait: purple flowers. However, this plant could still pass on the white flower factor to the next generation of plants.

5. Explain how Mendel's data supported his hypothesis. Support your answer by citing textual evidence from this lesson.

_____

_____

_____

_____

6. Mendel crossed a true-breeding plant with yellow peas with a true-breeding plant with green peas. All first generation offspring had yellow peas. Explain which trait is recessive.

_____

_____

_____

Relating Genetic Structure to Traits

Mendel's experiments and conclusions were the beginnings of scientific thought about how traits are passed from parents to offspring. Mendel's observations can be further explained by our modern understanding of the molecule called DNA. DNA is short for deoxyribonucleic acid. DNA contains instructions that help determine an organism's traits.

7. Where is DNA primarily located in a eukaryotic cell?

Only until scientists discovered the molecule DNA did they begin to truly understand the models Mendel developed about how traits are inherited.

Genes Influence Traits

DNA is organized into structures called **chromosomes.** An individual has paired sets of chromosomes. What Mendel called "factors" are now known as genes. A **gene** is a segment of the DNA located in the chromosomes of cells. Because an individual has pairs of chromosomes, an individual also has pairs of genes.

Each gene can have different forms, or variations. For example, Mendel's pea plants had two variations of the flower color gene, causing both purple and white flowers. Each parent contributes one set of genes to its offspring. So, for a particular trait, one gene variation comes from each parent. The different gene forms are called **alleles.** Alleles carry the codes for producing various **proteins,** which are large molecules that do much of the work in a cell and also make up much of the cell's structure. Proteins are responsible for most aspects of how our bodies function, as well as for our physical appearance and our behavior.

Mendel's pea plant traits were all controlled by just two alleles: a dominant one and a recessive one. For those pea plants, the allele for purple flowers is the dominant allele, and the allele for white flowers is the recessive allele. Some traits follow this inheritance pattern; however, most do not. Usually there are more than two alleles for a single gene within a population of organisms. Each organism, however, can carry only one or two alleles for one gene. Most traits, such as height and eye color, are not determined by only a single gene.

The Structure of DNA

The chemical components that make up DNA are too small to be observed directly. However, experiments and imaging techniques have helped scientists to infer the shape of DNA and the arrangement of its parts. A molecule of DNA is shaped like a twisted ladder, a shape that is called a *double helix*. The rungs of the ladder are made of a pair of bases. A stretch of base pairs along a DNA molecule is what makes up a gene. The instructions of DNA are coded in specific sequences of base pairs.

8. Describe the relationship between DNA, chromosomes, and genes.

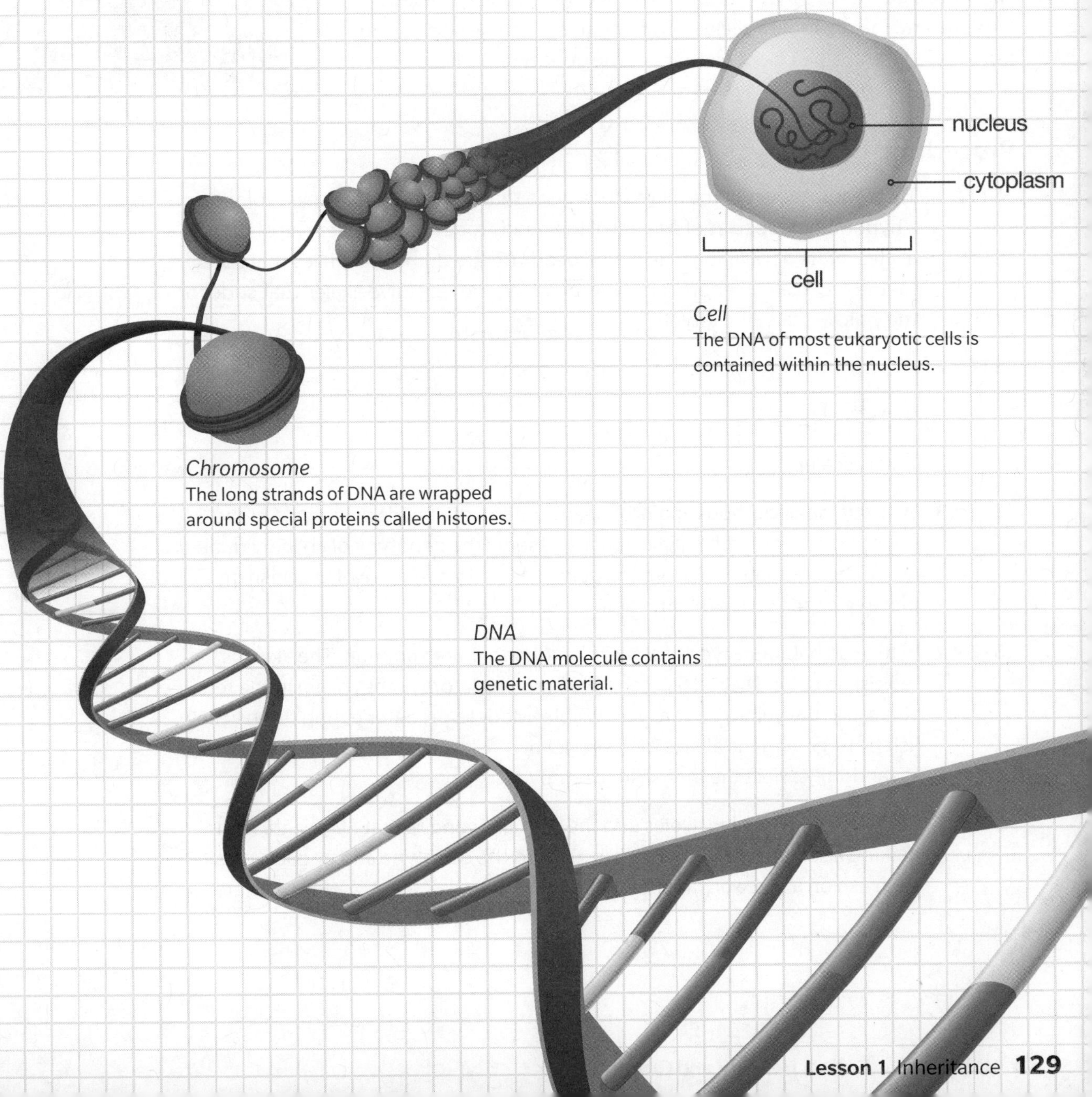

nucleus

cytoplasm

cell

Cell
The DNA of most eukaryotic cells is contained within the nucleus.

Chromosome
The long strands of DNA are wrapped around special proteins called histones.

DNA
The DNA molecule contains genetic material.

Hands-On Lab
Model Genes and Traits

Use a model to describe genetic variation for the scale color of a hypothetical fish species. Use evidence to predict over several generations the proportions of dominant and recessive alleles in the population.

The combination of alleles that an organism receives from its parents is called the organism's *genotype*. The observable traits of an organism are its *phenotype*. Genotypes are often represented by letter symbols. Often, dominant alleles are often shown with capital letters, and recessive alleles are shown with lowercase letters. For example, *F* could represent the dominant allele of purple flower color, and *f* could represent the recessive allele of white flower color in pea plants. You can write a genotype for a pea plant's flower color by using the letters to represent an individual's alleles. As an organism receives one allele from each parent, a pea plant might have the genotype *FF, Ff*, or *ff*.

Procedure

STEP 1 The beads represent the alleles for a gene that determines the scale color of a hypothetical species of fish. All of the beads together represent all of the alleles in the population of fish. Red beads (*R*) are dominant alleles that code for the red-scale phenotype. Yellow beads (*r*) are recessive alleles that code for the yellow-scale phenotype.

STEP 2 Write the genotype(s) for each phenotype.

Red scales: _____

Yellow scales: _____

STEP 3 Without looking, choose pairs of beads until all the beads are gone. Set the pairs of beads on a table. Each pair represents the genotype of an individual fish in the population. Record the genotype and phenotype of each fish on a piece of paper. This is the first generation.

STEP 4 In the fish habitat, a type of algae is becoming more common. The algae is reddish in color. The red fish can hide from predators as they swim in the red algae, but the yellow fish are very visible. Model a predator eating three yellow fish by removing the alleles for three yellow "fish" from the population. Be sure to randomly select the three fish to remove.

STEP 5 Replace the remaining alleles into the container and repeat Step 3, this time making a second generation of fish. Record the genotype and phenotype of each fish on a piece of paper.

Analysis

STEP 6 Compare the first- and second-generation phenotypes. Explain the reasons for any differences.

STEP 7 Predict what would happen after many generations if environmental conditions for these fish remained the same. Justify your response.

STEP 8 Suppose that yellow algae began to out-compete the red algae in the fish environment. Describe how you could model the next 2 generations of fish in this changed environment.

EVIDENCE NOTEBOOK

9. Compare the phenotypes of the fish scale color in this lab with the phenotypes of fur color in the kittens a the beginning of this lesson. Use evidence from the lab to explain why all of the kittens don't have the same fur color, even though they have the same parents.

Predict Effects of Mutation

Changes in a section of DNA are known as mutations. How do mutations happen? One cause of mutations is random errors that occur when DNA is being copied to make new cells. Mutations to DNA may be beneficial, neutral, or harmful.

A mutation might have a beneficial outcome to an organism by promoting resistance to a disease or a toxin or by allowing an organism to better use its food. A mutation might also have a harmful outcome, such as causing a genetic disease. Some mutations are neutral, such as when a mutation causes a change in eye or hair color, which does not affect the health of the individual. Some small changes in DNA do not change the proteins that the DNA codes for.

10. Suppose a gene mutation does not affect the protein that the gene codes for. What effect will the mutation have on the individual? Explain your reasoning.

_____

_____

_____

_____

_____

_____

Modeling Inheritance of Traits

Not all traits are passed on from parent to offspring. Some traits are learned, such as the ability to ride a bicycle or write your name in cursive. Other traits are acquired, or taken on after birth. For example, a person might dye his hair blue, but that is not an inherited trait.

Flower color is an inherited trait.

11. Engineer It The three processes below would allow a horticulturist to grow only purple-flowered pea plants for many generations. However, the horticulturist is constrained by time. Circle which of the following processes would allow the horticulturist to grow only purple-flowered plants in the shortest amount of time. Explain your reasoning below.

A. A horticulturist could start by crossing two plants with purple flowers. In each new generation, they should select plants with purple flowers to cross, until all of the plants for several generations in a row have purple flowers.

B. A horticulturist could develop a way to determine the flower color genotypes of the plants, and only cross plants that have the FF genotype.

C. A horticulturist could allow the purple plants to self-pollinate, then separate purple plants from the first generation and allow those plants to self-pollinate.

Genes Are Passed from Parents to Offspring

Even before anyone knew about DNA or genes, Mendel figured out that "factors"—what we now call genes—were passed from parent to offspring. **Inheritance** is the passing of genes from parents to offspring. In one form of reproduction, offspring inherit all of their genes from one parent so that the offspring and the parent are genetically identical. For example, you take a cutting of a houseplant and grow a whole new individual plant. The new plant is genetically identical to its parent unless mutations occur. In another form of reproduction, two parents contribute genetic material. The offspring of this type of reproduction are genetically different from each of the parents as well as from each other.

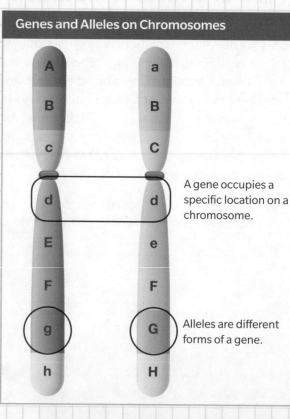

Genes and Alleles on Chromosomes

A gene occupies a specific location on a chromosome.

Alleles are different forms of a gene.

12. Mendel's peas had two phenotypes for pod color: yellow pods and green pods. The allele for yellow pod color is *Y* and the allele for green pod color is *y*. On the lines below, write the phenotype for each genotype. Then summarize how these alleles were passed from parent to offspring.

Genotype	Phenotype	Summary
Parent 1: *YY*	A. _____	
Parent 2: *yy*	B. _____	
All offpsring: *Yy*	C. _____	

Inheritance Is Modeled with Punnett Squares

When Gregor Mendel studied pea plants, he noticed that traits are inherited in patterns. One tool for understanding the basic patterns of heredity is a Punnett square. A *Punnett square* is a graphic used to predict the possible genotypes of offspring in a given cross. A Punnett square does not tell what the genotype of an offspring will definitely be. Instead, it shows the possible gene combinations (genotypes), and from that, you can find the probability of an offspring will have a particular genotype.

Recall that each parent has two alleles for a particular gene, and one of those alleles will be passed on to the offspring. So an offspring receives one allele from each parent. The genotype and phenotype of the offspring depends on which alleles of the parents combine during fertilization of the egg.

Let's look at a Punnett square for Mendel's pea plants. The example is for a cross between a pea plant with purple flowers (*FF*) and a pea plant with white flowers (*ff*). The top of the Punnett square shows the possible alleles for this trait in one parent (*F* and *F*). The left side shows the possible alleles for other parent (*f* and *f*). Each compartment within the Punnett square shows a possible allele combination for potential offspring.

Punnett Square for Flower Color
13. Fill in the missing genotype to complete the Punnett square.

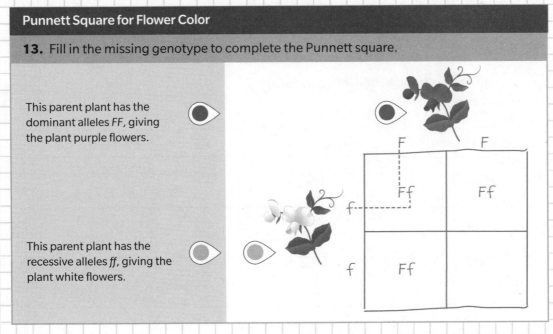

This parent plant has the dominant alleles *FF*, giving the plant purple flowers.

This parent plant has the recessive alleles *ff*, giving the plant white flowers.

14. Summarize the predicted genotypes and phenotypes shown in the Punnett square above.

15. Many traits, such as fur color, are determined by more than one gene. How might the influence of multiple genes affect the range of possible phenotypes for fur color? Record your evidence.

Do the Math

Calculate Genotype Probability

Recall that a Punnett square shows all possible genotypes for the offspring of a cross, not what the exact results of the cross will be. A Punnett square tells the probability that an offspring will have a certain genotype. *Probability* is the mathematical chance of a specific outcome in relation to the total number of possible outcomes.

Probability can be expressed as a ratio, an expression that compares two quantities. A ratio written as 1:4 is read as "one to four." Punnett square ratios show the probability that any one offspring will get certain alleles. Probability can be expressed as a percentage, too. A percentage compares a number to 100, stating the number of times a certain outcome might happen out of a hundred chances.

16. Fill in the right column of the Punnett square. The allele for red feathers (*R*) is dominant and the allele for brown feathers (*r*) is recessive. Both parents have a genotype *Rr* and have red feathers.

	R	r
R	RR	
r	Rr	

17. Write the probability for an offspring of this cross to have each genotype or phenotype:

Genotype or Phenotype	Probability	Percent of Chance
RR genotype	1:4	$1 \div 4 = 0.25$ $0.25 \times 100 = 25\%$
Rr genotype		
rr genotype		
red feathers		
brown feathers		

Continue Your Exploration

Name: _____   Date: _____

Check out the path below or go online to choose one of the other paths shown.

People in Science

- **Hands-On Labs** 🖐
- **Genetic Engineering**
- **Propose Your Own Path**

Go online to choose one of these other paths.

In the mid-19th century, scientists knew that the DNA molecule existed, but they did not know what it looked like. Many scientists studied DNA's structure, and the combined work of four scientists in particular helped solve the mystery.

DNA is made up of chemical compounds called *nucleotides*. A nucleotide consists of a sugar, a phosphate, and a base: thymine, guanine, adenine, or cytosine. Erwin Chargaff found that in DNA, the amount of adenine equals the amount of thymine and the amount of guanine equals the amount of cytosine.

Rosalind Franklin used x-ray diffraction to make images of the DNA molecule; her research indicated DNA had a spiral shape. James Watson and Francis Crick used Chargaff's and Franklin's research to build a model of DNA. In their model, DNA is in the shape of a double helix, which looks like a twisted ladder. The sugars and phosphates make up the outsides of the ladder, while the "rungs" are made up of joined pairs of nucleotides. Adenine (A) pairs with thymine (T), and guanine (G) pairs with cytosine (C). These paired, or complementary, bases fit together like two pieces of a puzzle.

T

C

A

G

Continue Your Exploration

1. A scientist knows that a molecule of DNA is 27% cytosine. What else does the scientist know about the DNA molecule? Choose the correct answer.

   A. The DNA molecule is 27% guanine.

   B. The DNA molecule is 27% adenine.

   C. The DNA molecule is 73% guanine.

   D. The DNA molecule is 27% thymine.

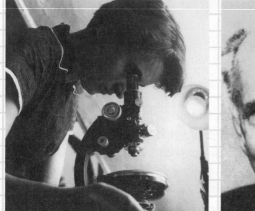
X-ray crystallographer Rosalind Franklin, circa 1942.

Biochemist Erwin Chargaff, circa 1970.

James Watson (left) and Francis Crick (right), in their laboratory, circa 1953.

2. Describe how the contributions of Rosalind Franklin and Erwin Chargaff lead to the discovery of the structure of DNA by James Watson and Francis Crick.

3. Suppose that one side of a segment of DNA had the bases ATCGGA. What would the bases be on the other complementary half of the DNA molecule?

   A. ATCGGA

   B. CGATTC

   C. AGGCTA

   D. TAGCCT

4. **Collaborate** Work with classmates to build a model of DNA that you could use to teach others about how the bases pair together.

Can You Explain It?

Name: _____   **Date:** _____

Look again at the picture of the kittens.

How do you think these kittens got their fur colors?

EVIDENCE NOTEBOOK

Refer to your notes in your Evidence Notebook to help you construct an explanation for how these kittens got their fur colors.

1. State your claim. Make sure your claim fully explains how the kittens got their fur colors.

2. Summarize the evidence you have gathered to support your claim and explain your reasoning.

Checkpoints

Answer the following questions to check your understanding of the lesson.

Use the diagram to answer questions 3 and 4.

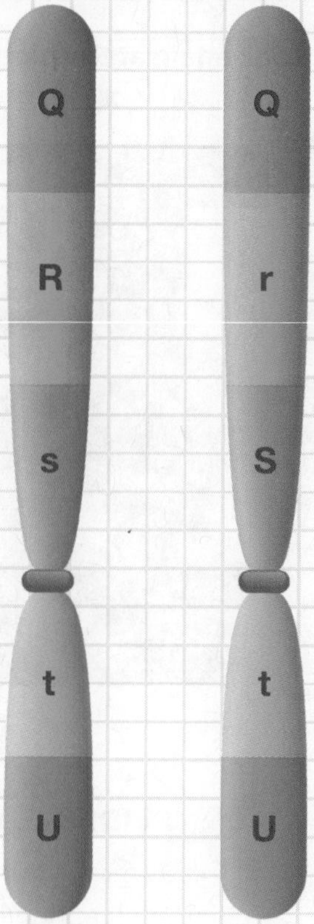

3. For which gene or genes will the recessive trait be expressed in this individual? Choose all that apply.

    A. The Q gene

    B. The S gene

    C. The T gene

    D. The U gene

4. What genotype(s) might the parents of this individual have for the Q gene? Select all that apply.

    A. QQ

    B. Qq

    C. qq

Use the diagram to answer Questions 5 and 6.

5. For Mendel's peas, seed shape can be round (*R*) or wrinkled (*r*). Fill in all of the possible genotypes that could result from the cross shown in this Punnett square.

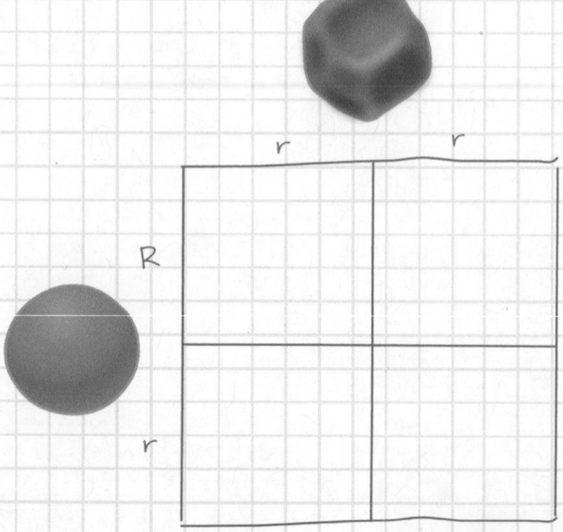

6. Use the information from the seed shape Punnett square. Circle the correct percent of chance to complete the sentence.

    An offspring from this cross has a
    0% / 25% / 50% / 75% / 100%
    chance of having round peas and a
    0% / 25% / 50% / 75% / 100%
    chance of having wrinkled peas.

Interactive Review

Complete this section to review the main concepts of the lesson.

Mendel figured out a basic inheritance pattern by studying pea plants.

A. Mendel studied seven different features of pea plants including flower color, seed shape, and seed color. Describe the evidence Mendel used to determine if a particular trait was dominant or recessive.

DNA contains the alleles of genes, which determine traits.

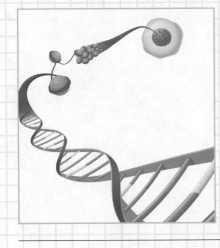

B. Explain how chromosomes, genes, and alleles are related.

Some traits are inherited. Others are learned or acquired.

C. For Mendel's peas, yellow seed color (*G*) is dominant and green seed color (*g*) is recessive. Write and complete a Punnett square to model a cross between a heterozygous parent (*Gg*) and a recessive parent (*gg*).

Asexual and Sexual Reproduction

Female grizzly bears have a litter of one to four cubs. The cubs will stay with their mother for two to three years.

By the end of this lesson . . .

you will be able to describe how reproduction relates to genetic diversity.

Go *online* to view the digital version of the Hands-On Lab for this lesson and to download additional lab resources.

CAN YOU EXPLAIN IT?

Why do this mother and baby horse look different?

Appaloosa horses are known for their distinctive coat patterns. The color of the coats can be brown, black, white, gray, chestnut, or a combination of two or more of those colors.

1. Look at the coat colors and patterns of the mother and the foal. How do you think the horses get these combinations of color and patterns?

 EVIDENCE NOTEBOOK As you explore the lesson, gather evidence to help you explain why some organisms look like their parents and others do not.

Describing Types of Reproduction

Earth is home to millions of species of plants, animals, and other living things. In order for a species to survive, individual organisms of that species must make more organisms like themselves. Organisms produce **offspring**, or young organisms like themselves. Reproduction—the process by which organisms generate a new individual of the same species—is a characteristic of all living things. During the process of reproduction, organisms pass genetic material to their offspring.

Parents and Offspring

Thornback ray and pup
Thornback ray females lay fertilized eggs in sand or gravel in shallow waters. The eggs hatch into pups after 4–6 months.

Luna moth and caterpillar
Luna moth caterpillars hatch from eggs. After 3–4 weeks of feeding, they spin a cocoon of silk. They emerge as adults after 2–3 weeks.

Teddy bear cactus and clones
Teddy bear cactus branches can stick to the fur of animals. The branches fall off the traveling animal and grow as a clone plant.

Green frog and tadpole
Frogs lay eggs in water. Tadpoles hatch from the eggs. After about 12 weeks of development, they are ready to leave the water as adult frogs.

2. **Discuss** Does the offspring resemble the parent? With a partner, discuss the ways the parents and offspring are similar and the ways they are different.

Types of Reproduction

The two main forms of reproduction are asexual reproduction and sexual reproduction. In **asexual reproduction**, a single individual is the parent. The parent passes copies of its genes to its offspring, so the offspring are genetically identical to the parent unless mutations occur. Most unicellular organisms reproduce asexually. Fungi, plants, and some animals can reproduce asexually. Asexual reproduction allows an organism to reproduce quickly and can produce a large number of offspring in a short period of time.

3. How many parents are involved in the reproduction of each bacterium?

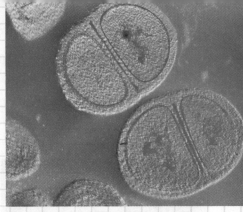

These bacteria reproduce by means of binary fission. During binary fission, an organism makes a copy of its DNA and then splits in two.

In **sexual reproduction**, there are two parents. Each parent contributes half of its genetic information to the offspring, so the offspring are genetically different from both parents. Most multicellular organisms reproduce sexually, including plants and animals. Sexual reproduction takes more time and produces fewer offspring than asexual reproduction. However, sexual reproduction increases genetic variation. This variation increases the chance that some offspring will have new traits that will help them survive a changing environment.

4. How many parents are involved in the reproduction of this flowering plant?

Some organisms can reproduce both asexually and sexually, depending on environmental conditions and other factors. Organisms that can use both types of reproduction include fungi, many plants, some reptiles and fish, and a few types of insects.

5. Redwood trees can reproduce both sexually and asexually. Which type of reproduction do you think a redwood might be an advantage if a large clearing around the tree became available?

This coral dahlia flower has male and female parts. The male parts make pollen, which contains male reproductive cells. Pollen from one flower can be transferred to the female part of another flower, beginning the process of reproduction.

© Houghton Mifflin Harcourt • Image Credits: (t) ©CNRI/Science Source; (b) ©Dirk Herdramm/EyeEm/Getty Images

EVIDENCE NOTEBOOK

6. Horses reproduce sexually. How many parents does the foal have? Where does the foal's genetic information come from?

7. Read about the reproductive processes of the animals below. Then decide whether the process is an example of asexual reproduction, sexual reproduction, or both.

	Male bluegills create nests for female bluegills to lay their eggs. The male bluegills fertilize the eggs with their sperm. Male bluegills guard the eggs until they hatch.	
	Male and female jellyfish release sperm and eggs into the water. A fertilized egg develops into a larva that will grow into a polyp. The polyp will release a portion of its body in a process called budding. The bud will grow into an adult jellyfish.	
	Corals release eggs and sperm into the water. Fertilized eggs develop into larva, which attach to surfaces and grow into polyps (adult corals). New coral polyps also can bud off and remain attached to their parents. Or, part of a coral can break off and grow into a new coral.	

Engineer It

Develop a Hybrid

Gardeners often breed two different varieties of a plant to produce offspring with desirable traits. These plants are called hybrids. The gardener selects parents with traits that are desired in the offspring, such as flower color, plant height, fruit yield, or pest resistance.

There are thousands of rose hybrids in nearly every color and a variety of shapes.

8. A gardener would like to produce a hybrid that is tall and has a red flower color. Describe how the gardener might try to produce this hybrid.

_____

_____

_____

_____

_____

_____

Relating Reproduction to Genetic Variation

Reproduction is the process by which organisms inherit genes, which are segments of DNA on a chromosome. The genes inherited from the parent or parents determine the genetic traits of offspring. When an organism reproduces asexually, all the genetic material of the offspring is inherited from one parent. When an organism reproduces sexually, the offspring receives half of its genes from each parent.

Look at the photos of the hydra and the amphibian. Although hydras sometimes reproduce sexually, they reproduce mainly by *budding*, a type of asexual reproduction. A bud begins to grow on an adult's body. When it has developed a mouth and tentacles, the bud breaks off from the adult. Amphibians reproduce sexually. Female adult amphibians lay eggs that are fertilized by sperm from adult male amphibians.

9. **Discuss** With a partner, reread the descriptions of the reproductive process of the two organisms. Do you think the offspring of each organism are genetically identical to the parent or not genetically identical to the parent? Support your argument with evidence.

A hydra is an animal that lives in freshwater. Its body is shaped like a tube. It has tentacles around its mouth.

An amphibian is an animal that lives both on land and in water.

Inheritance and Asexual Reproduction

Prokaryotes, such as bacteria, are unicellular and reproduce by a type of cell division called *binary fission*. This process results in two unicellular organisms that are genetically identical to the parent. Asexual reproduction in multicellular organisms is a little more involved. But it also usually involves a type of cell division that results in genetically identical cells.

Having offspring that are genetically identical to the parent ensures that any favorable traits that the parent has are passed on to the offspring. However, if the environment changes, a population with low genetic variation is less likely to have individuals with traits that allow them to survive.

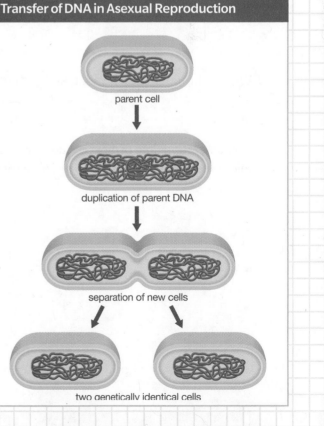

Transfer of DNA in Asexual Reproduction

parent cell

duplication of parent DNA

separation of new cells

two genetically identical cells

Do the Math

Calculate the Rate of Asexual Reproduction

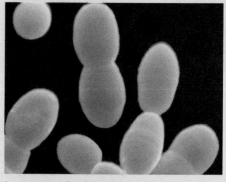

Lactococcus lactis is a bacteria used commonly in the production of cheese.

Generation time is the average time between two generations in a population. For example, if a certain type of bacteria reproduces every 20 minutes, then the generation time is 20 minutes. Since bacteria reproduce by dividing into two cells, a bacteria population can double in a generation time.

10. Use the data from the table to create a line graph of the bacteria population over time.

Time (in minutes)	Number of *Lactococcus lactis* Cells
0	1
52	2
104	4
156	8
208	16
260	32
312	64

11. What is the independent variable? What is the dependent variable?

12. The generation time of most bacteria can be measured in minutes. What advantage might there be in being able to reproduce very rapidly?

13. If bacteria cells can reproduce so fast, then why don't bacteria take over the world?

Inheritance and Sexual Reproduction

Sexual reproduction requires two parents. Each parent produces **gametes**, or sex cells. In animals, many plants, algae, and fungi, female organisms produce eggs and male organisms produce sperm cells. Gametes have half the total number of chromosomes, one copy of each chromosome. The parent gametes are all genetically different.

During sexual reproduction, a sperm cell and an egg join in a process called *fertilization*. When an egg is fertilized by a sperm cell, a new, genetically different cell is formed. This cell—called a *zygote*— has a complete set of genetic material because it has received half of its chromosomes from one parent and half from the other parent. Thus, the zygote has inherited two copies of each gene, one from each parent. The genes may be identical, or they may differ from one another. The zygote will go through many cell divisions to form an organism that is genetically different from both parents.

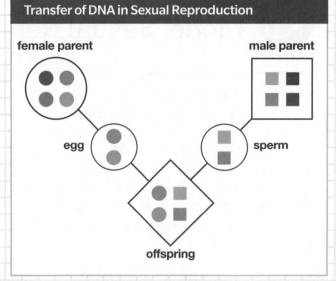

Transfer of DNA in Sexual Reproduction

14. What other genetic combinations might be possible from the parent organisms shown in the diagram? Circle the letter of all possibilities that apply.

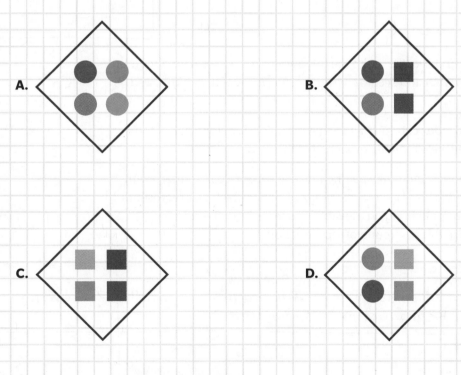

Advantages of Genetic Variation

Sexual reproduction increases genetic variation in a population of organisms. Offspring have different traits from their parents and from each other. This genetic variation improves the chance that at least some individuals will survive. If the environment changes, a population with greater genetic variation is more likely to have individuals with traits that will allow them to survive new conditions.

Model Sexual Reproduction

You will model genetic variation in a sexually reproducing organism. Then you will compare the results to probabilities predicted using a Punnett square.

In cats, the allele for short hair is dominant and the allele for long hair is recessive. You will use a Punnett square to predict the genotypes of the kittens that can result in a cross between a short-haired cat and a long-haired cat. Short hair will be represented by *H*. Long hair will be represented by *h*. You can review Punnett squares in the Inheritance lesson.

MATERIALS
- index cards, colored (10)
- index cards, white (10)
- pen
- scissors

Procedure and Analysis

STEP 1 Complete the Punnett square.

STEP 2 What percentage of offspring are predicted to have short hair using this model? What percentage are predicted to have long hair?

	H	h
h		
h		

STEP 3 On the 10 colored index cards, write the genotype of the short-haired mother cat, *Hh*. On the 10 white index cards, write the genotype of the long-haired father cat, *hh*.

STEP 4 Cut each of the 20 index cards in half so that one allele is on one half of the card and the other allele is on the other half of the card.

STEP 5 Model reproduction by randomly pairing one allele from a colored card with one allele from a white card to create 20 pairs of alleles. Each pair represents the genotype for one offspring. In the table, record the number of each genotype formed in this first round of reproduction.

Offspring Genotypes	First Round of Reproduction	Second Round of Reproduction	Total	Percentage
HH				
Hh				
hh				

© Houghton Mifflin Harcourt

STEP 6 Mix up the allele cards and repeat Step 5 to model a second round of reproduction. Record your results in your data table.

STEP 7 Add the results from the first and second rounds of reproduction to find the total number of times each genotype was formed. Record your results.

STEP 8 Create a bar graph that shows the total number of each genotype formed.

STEP 9 Divide the total for each genotype by 40 (the total number of pairs formed) and multiply by 100 to find the percentage of each genotype. Record this data in the table.

STEP 10 **Discuss** How do the genotype percentages predicted in your Punnett square compare to the results of your modeling experiment with the index cards? Share your data with other groups and compare results.

EVIDENCE NOTEBOOK

15. Look back at the photo of the horse and foal at the beginning of the lesson. Is the foal genetically identical or not identical to either parent? How do you think the coat colors and patterns relate to the allele possibilities?

Language SmArts
Compare Asexual and Sexual Reproduction

16. Compare asexual reproduction and sexual reproduction by completing the Venn diagram with phrases from the Word Bank.

- one parent
- two parents
- produces offspring
- genetic variation

- fast
- slow
- many offspring
- few offspring

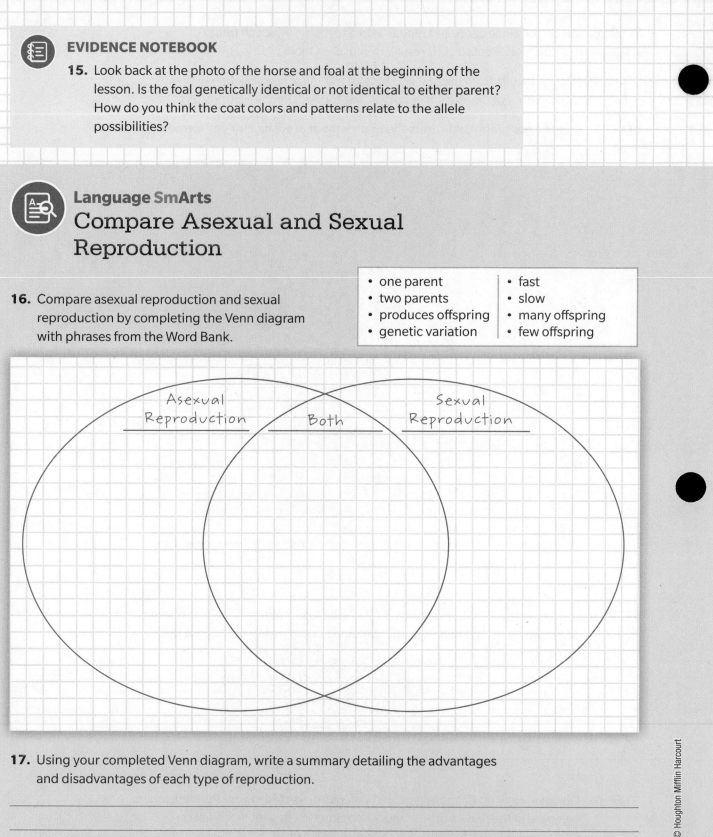

Asexual Reproduction   Both   Sexual Reproduction

17. Using your completed Venn diagram, write a summary detailing the advantages and disadvantages of each type of reproduction.

_____

_____

_____

_____

© Houghton Mifflin Harcourt

Continue Your Exploration

Name: _____   Date: _____

Check out the path below or go online to choose one of the other paths shown.

Factors That Influence Reproduction

- **Hands-On Labs** ✋
- **Odd Reproduction**
- **Propose Your Own Path**

Go online to choose one of these other paths.

> Nearly every multicellular organism on Earth can reproduce by sexual reproduction. But some organisms are able to reproduce both asexually and sexually. Organisms that can use both types of reproduction are able to reproduce successfully even when environmental conditions are unfavorable or mating partners are not available. Other factors influence the mode of reproduction used by these organisms.

Honeybee reproduction occurs when a queen bee mates with a male bee, called a drone. The queen is the only female bee that mates. She uses the drone's sperm to fertilize eggs that will develop into female worker bees. An average colony has between 20,000 and 80,000 workers. The queen can also lay unfertilized eggs that will develop into drones. An average colony has between 300 and 800 drones.

1. How is this method of reproduction advantageous to the honeybee colony? Select all that apply.

   A. The queen bee is the only member of the hive that is the result of sexual reproduction.

   B. Sexually produced worker bees have genetic diversity, which could increase their overall fitness.

   C. Male bees are not necessary for the colony to function and can be produced only when needed for mating.

Continue Your Exploration

Fungi are multicellular organisms that can live anywhere there is decaying matter, but most species of fungi are associated with trees. Fungi often reproduce asexually by releasing spores, which are reproductive cells that can develop into a new individual without fusing with another reproductive cell. They can also reproduce asexually by budding. They can reproduce sexually when spores from two parents fuse.

2. Describe how environmental changes might affect the type of reproduction utilized by fungi. Relate the type of reproduction to genetic variation of offspring in your answer.

Strawberry plants can reproduce sexually by producing fruit or asexually by sending out runners. Runners are extensions of the central stem of the plant that spread out along the ground and grow into new strawberry plants.

3. What is the advantage of sending out many runners from the central stem? What is the disadvantage to the central plant?

4. **Collaborate** Other organisms that can reproduce both sexually and asexually include Komodo dragons, stick insects, ginger plants, and yeasts. With a classmate select one of these species and research its reproductive strategies. Under what conditions does the organism use the different modes of reproduction? Present your findings in a poster or presentation.

Can You Explain It?

Name: _____   Date: _____

Look at the photo and compare the coat color and pattern of the Appaloosa foal to its mother's.

Why do this mother and baby horse look different?

EVIDENCE NOTEBOOK

Refer to the notes in your Evidence Notebook to help you construct an explanation for why this foal looks different than its mother.

1. State your claim. Make sure your claim fully explains why the foal's coat does not look exactly like its mother's coat.

2. Summarize the evidence you have gathered to support your claim and explain your reasoning.

Lesson 2 Asexual and Sexual Reproduction **153**

Checkpoints

Answer the following questions to check your understanding of the lesson.

3. Marmosets usually give birth to fraternal twins, two offspring that grow from two different fertilized eggs. Marmoset twins are genetically identical / not identical.

4. What advantage does the white-faced marmoset gain by its method of reproduction? Select all that apply.

   A. genetic variation

   B. larger number of offspring

   C. ability to colonize an area quickly

   D. ability to adapt to changes to its environment

A white-faced marmoset protects her fraternal twin pups.

5. Dandelions can produce seeds by both asexual and sexual reproduction. How does this benefit the dandelion? Select all that apply.

   A. The sexually produced plants provide genetic diversity to the population.

   B. The asexually produced plants ensure that favorable traits are passed to the offspring.

   C. The sexually produced plants do not compete with the asexually produced plants.

   D. The asexually produced plants can rapidly colonize an area.

6. If you pull a dandelion plant out of the ground, a new dandelion plant can grow from fragments of the deep taproot that may be left behind. Under which environmental conditions might this be advantageous? Select all that apply.

   A. warm surface conditions

   B. dry surface conditions

   C. cold surface conditions

   D. wet surface conditions

A young dandelion flower (yellow florets) grows next to a mature flower with a full seed head.

Interactive Review

Complete this section to review the main concepts of the lesson.

Two types of reproduction are asexual reproduction, which involves one parent, and sexual reproduction, which involves two parents.

A. If an organism lives in an area where there are not many other members of its species, which form of reproduction might be advantageous? Explain.

Asexual reproduction results in offspring that are genetically identical to the parent. Sexual reproduction results in offspring that have a combination of genes from each parent.

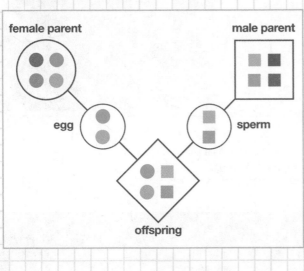

female parent

male parent

egg

sperm

offspring

B. Make a Venn diagram to compare and contrast asexual reproduction with sexual reproduction.

Plant Reproduction and Growth

The moth orchid, which grows in South Eastern Asia and Australia, has flowers that bloom for three months.

By the end of this lesson . . .

you will be able to explain how genetic and environmental factors affect the growth and reproduction of plants.

© Houghton Mifflin Harcourt • Image Credits: ©Jean-Michel Volat/Moment/Getty Images

Go online to view the digital version of the Hands-On Lab for this lesson and to download additional lab resources.

CAN YOU EXPLAIN IT?

How does the structure of the sacred lotus flower relate to reproduction?

The sacred lotus grows in soil that is submerged in water. An individual plant can live for a thousand years, and the seeds can remain viable for as long as 1,300 years.

Researchers have found that the sacred lotus has the ability to regulate the temperature of its flowers. As the air temperature cools, the flower maintains a steady temperature and emits a fragrant scent.

1. What function do you think a flower that stays warm at night might have for a plant? What function do you think a sweet smelling flower might have for a plant?

 EVIDENCE NOTEBOOK As you explore the lesson, gather evidence to help you explain the function of the sacred lotus flower.

Investigating Reproductive Structures of Plants

Like all living organisms, plants use the process of reproduction to produce offspring. Different species have different ways of reproducing, but they all have specialized structures for reproduction. These structures come in a wide variety of colors, shapes, and sizes. They can be a source of nutrition for animals, and objects of beauty highly valued by people.

Analyze Plant Structures

2. Examine the plant structures below. Which functions do you think each structure plays in the plant's reproduction? Write the functions for each plant.

attract animals	disperse seeds
protect seeds	

	Willow trees have flower clusters called catkins that can be male or female. The female catkins contain seeds, and they are covered with long, fluffy hairs.	
	Cherry trees have distinctive flowers that range in color from white to pink. The flowers contain sugary nectar and protein-rich pollen.	
	Pomegranate trees grow in warm, dry climates. Their seeds are housed inside colorful, juicy fruits.	
	Blue spruce trees have male and female cones, both of which are covered with tough scales. These female cones contain lightweight seeds.	

Sexual Reproduction in Plants

All plants can reproduce sexually. Plants produced by sexual reproduction are genetically different from both parents and from each other. This genetic variation increases the chance that some offspring will have traits that help them survive in a changing environment.

Reproduction of Seedless Plants

Seedless plants do not produce seeds for reproduction. Instead of seeds, the bodies of seedless plants grow from spores. A *spore* of a seedless plant is a tiny structure that is dispersed from the parent plant and can grow into a new plant body. A sperm from one plant must swim through water to fertilize the egg of another plant. Because of this requirement for water, many seedless plants live in moist environments. A fertilized egg grows into a stalk-like structure that produces spores, and the life cycle continues.

Reproductive Structures of Seedless Plants

Mosses are seedless plants that grow on rocks, soil, trees, and even between cracks in pavement.

Release of Spores
Under the right conditions, spores are released from this part of the moss plant, called a *capsule*. Spores may land far away from the parent plant and grow into a new plant body.

Fertilization
In this part of the plant, fertilization occurs when a sperm swims to an egg. A fertilized egg then grows into a stalk-like structure, on which spores are produced.

3. **Discuss** How might dry conditions affect the reproductive success of a seedless plant?

Reproduction of Seed Plants

In seed plants, sperm are carried in a microscopic structure called pollen. *Pollen* looks like fine dust and can be transported by wind, water, and animals. Eggs develop inside a structure called an *ovule*. The ovule has a small opening where transported pollen can get inside. When pollen reaches and fertilizes an egg, **pollination** occurs.

A fertilized egg develops into an embryo. The embryo will then grow into a new plant. The ovule becomes the **seed**, the structure that contains the embryo inside a protective coating. Seeds can be distributed away from the parent plant by wind, water, or animals. After seeds have been dispersed, they will grow into new plants.

Seed plants can be classified as nonflowering or flowering. Nonflowering plants produce seeds that are not enclosed in a fruit. Most non-flowering seed plants produce seeds enclosed in a structure called a *cone*. Flowering plants produce flowers and fruit. Flowering plants are the largest group within the Plantae kingdom. They are also the largest group of plants that live on land.

Reproductive Structures of Non-Flowering Seed Plants

Conifers are non-flowering plants that produce male and female cones.

Male Cone Pollen sacs are located on the scales of the male cone. Pollen is produced here. Mature male cones release pollen into the air. Pollen often travels by wind.

Female Cone The female cone has a pair of ovules on each scale. Pollination occurs when pollen reaches an egg inside an ovule. After they are pollinated, the fertilized eggs will develop into seeds. The seeds are dispersed when the cone breaks apart.

4. Based on the structure of the seeds below, decide if the method of dispersal is wind, water, or animals. Then describe your evidence. Write the answer in the space provided.

Seed Structure	Dispersal Method
milkweed seedlings	
dry burdock	
palm seed	

EVIDENCE NOTEBOOK

5. The sacred lotus has a large seed pod that eventually dries out and causes the flower to bend over. How do you think the sacred lotus flower seeds are dispersed?

Asexual Reproduction in Plants

Many plants are also able to reproduce asexually. For example, in some plants a part of the parent plant, such as a root or a stem, can grow into a new plant. Tubers, such as potatoes, can sprout roots that take hold in the soil and produce a new plant. Other plants, such as spider plants, produce plantlets. *Plantlets* are tiny plants that grow along the edges of a plant's leaves. They eventually break off and develop into new plants. Asexual reproduction allows a plant to reproduce and colonize an area quickly.

Each "eye" on this potato is an asexual structure that can grow into a new plant.

6. Write *asexual reproduction* or *sexual reproduction* to indicate the type of reproduction that would be most advantageous in each environmental condition shown in the table below. Support your answers with reasoning.

Environmental Condition	Type of Reproduction	Reasoning
Sunlight and nutrient levels are stable.		
Water becomes scarce.		
A pest species is introduced.		
A new space for growth becomes available.		

Language SmArts
Write an Argument

7. The majority of plants on Earth are seed plants. Use evidence to construct an argument about why producing seeds might be advantageous to the reproductive success of a plant species.

_____

_____

_____

_____

_____

Analyzing Reproductive Success of Flowering Plants

Plants cannot move around to find mates or to deposit their seeds in the perfect spot for growth. Wind and water can assist plant reproduction. However, many plants rely on insects, birds, or mammals to carry their pollen and seeds.

Explore ONLINE!

The hawk moth visits flowers at night.

8. Night-blooming plants are usually pollinated by animals that are active at night, such as some species of beetles, moths, and bats. What characteristics might a night-blooming flower have to attract nighttime feeders?

Pollination in Flowering Plants

Recall that the sperm of seed plants is carried in pollen. When pollen reaches an egg of the same kind of plant, it is called *pollination*. Some types of plants usually self-pollinate. This means that pollen is transferred to the egg of the same plant. Other types of plants usually cross-pollinate. In this case, the pollen from one plant is transferred to the egg of another plant. Animal pollinators play an important role in cross-pollination of plants.

Flowers contain nectar, a sugar-rich liquid that provides energy and nutrients to animals. Animals attracted to the flowers by their color or scent are rewarded with a tasty meal of nectar. The plant benefits because the animal carries away pollen that sticks to its body. The pollen is deposited on the next flower the animal visits.

9. **Discuss** Why might it be beneficial for a plant to be able to self-pollinate and to also have adaptations that attract animal pollinators?

Explore Reproduction in a Flowering Plant

The structures of the reproductive organs found in a flower relate to their function in pollination.

Stamen The stamen is a flower's male reproductive structure. A stamen consists of an anther, the pollen-producing part of the flower. The anther sits on top of a thin stalk. The anther produces spores that develop into pollen.

Pistil The pistil is the female reproductive structure of a flower. A pistil consists of the stigma, the style, and the ovary. The stigma is often sticky or covered in hairs. This makes it easier to collect pollen. The ovary contains the ovules, which produce eggs. After fertilization, the ovules develop into seeds. The ovary develops into a fruit.

Pollinator As pollinators feed on nectar, pollen, and fruit, pollen from a flower's anther rubs off on their bodies. When they fly to a second flower, pollen from the first flower rubs off on the second flower's stigma. Meanwhile, pollen from the second flower's anther rubs off on the pollinators' bodies, ready to be delivered to another flower.

heliconia flower

Heliconia is found in the rain forests of Central America and southern Mexico.

10. Based on the structure of the heliconia flower, which animal do you think is its pollinator?

A.

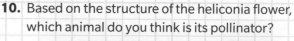

long-nosed bat

B.

hercules beetle

C.

green hermit hummingbird

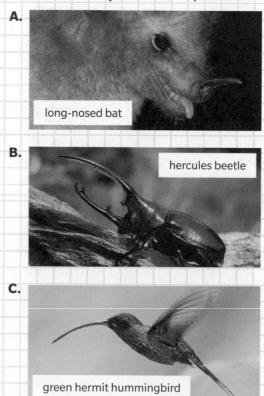

Hands-On Lab
Investigate Flower Structures

A flower contains the male and reproductive structures of a flowering plant. In addition, flowers have specialized leaves called sepals and petals. Sepals cover and protect the flower while it is budding. Petals are often colorful and can help attract animal pollinators. The pedicel is part of the stem supports the flower. At the end of the pedicel is a receptacle, which forms the base of the flower. You will dissect a flower and record drawings of the structures you discover.

MATERIALS
- flower
- hand lens
- lab gloves (as needed for allergies)
- scalpel
- surgical mask (as needed for allergies)

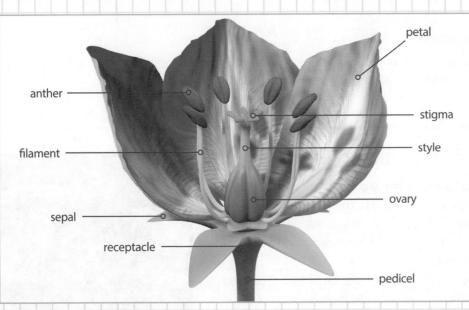

Procedure

STEP 1 Use the scalpel to carefully dissect the flower. Sort the structures.

STEP 2 **Draw** Use the hand lens to examine each structure. Draw and label one example of each structure. Depending on the type of flower you dissect, the structures of your flower might look different than the structures in the illustration.

Analysis and Conclusions

STEP 3 Describe patterns you observed in the arrangement of the flower parts.

STEP 4 **Collaborate** With a partner, discuss the body features you would expect of an animal that pollinates the type of flower you dissected.

EVIDENCE NOTEBOOK

11. The sacred lotus plant is pollinated by bees and beetles. How do the characteristics of the sacred lotus flower help attract these pollinators?

Seed Dispersal of Flowering Plants

Wind and water disperse the seeds of many plants. Animals also play a role in seed dispersal. Animals are attracted to the tasty fruits of some flowering plants. When an animal eats a fruit, the seeds pass through the animal's digestive system. The seeds are then deposited away from the parent plant as the animal travels.

Other types of seeds can hitch a ride on the fur or feet of passing animals. The seeds have hooks, barbs, or sticky mucus that allows them to attach to animals.

Some animals bury the seeds of plants, planning to return and eat them later. If an animal does not retrieve the buried seed, the seeds will germinate where they are buried. Squirrels that bury oak tree acorns are a good example of this type of animal-assisted seed dispersal.

12. In what ways might the dispersal of seeds far from the parent plant be advantageous for the survival of the offspring?

13. Many animals that disperse plant seeds are birds or mammals. Some insects and fish also spread seeds. Ants, for example, carry seeds underground. How might this method of dispersal help seeds survive?

This bird will excrete the prickly pear seeds through its digestive system.

Burrs stick to the fur and feet of mammals, like this horse.

Do the Math
Analyze Colony Collapse Disorder

Bees are important pollinators for the global food supply. In the United States $15 billion a year in crops, such as apples, berries, almonds, and cucumbers, are pollinated by bees. However, for at least a decade, bees have been suffering from a syndrome known as colony collapse disorder (CCD). Scientists are investigating various causes of CCD. Factors related to CCD include bacteria, parasites, pesticides use, and habitat destruction.

U.S.–Managed Honeybee Colony Loss

This figure shows estimates of the honeybee losses over a winter season (October 1, 2014– April 1, 2015), and for an entire year (April 1, 2014–April 1, 2015).

14. What is the average percentage loss of bees across the 49 states shown in the map, from April 2014 to April 2015?

_____

_____

_____

15. Which five U.S. states lost the highest percentage of bees? Which five states (not including Alaska) lost the lowest percentage of bees? What possible questions for further research are suggested by this data?

_____

_____

_____

_____

_____

Describing Factors that Affect Plant Growth

Plants need air, sunlight, water, space, and nutrients for growth. Each plant species has its own specific requirements. Some plants need special conditions for seeds to grow into plants, or *germinate*. For example, water is important for some seed germination. The seeds of some plants will germinate only after a rainfall or during the rainy season. Temperature is another factor that affects seed germination. Some seeds will germinate only after being exposed to cold temperatures for long periods. Some seeds need to experience extreme heat, such as high temperatures produced by a forest fire. The extreme temperatures help break down the tough seed coat.

16. How might passing through an animal's digestive system help the germination of some types of seeds?

Dutch iris seeds need cold temperatures to grow.

Genetic Factors Affect Plant Growth

Genetic factors are the specific forms of genes that parents pass on to offspring during reproduction. A plant's genes affect its traits. Therefore, different genes are responsible for the differences in the thousands of plant types, or species, that exist on Earth. For example, ferns grow well in the moist, low-light conditions of the forest floor, and cacti grow well in dry, full-light conditions. The ability of different types of plants to grow in such different conditions is due to genetic differences between plant species.

Individual plants of the same species can also have genetic differences. These differences exist because there can be different forms of the same gene. For example, different varieties of the same plant species may grow at different rates, even if they are planted in the same garden. Different forms of certain plant genes may affect drought tolerance or leaf size, both of which can affect the growth of plants.

Engineer It
Explore Plant Hybrids

Plant breeders cross-pollinate different types of plants in order to produce a desired trait or traits in the offspring. For instance, they might try to introduce resistance to disease, drought, or pests. Breeders also select for flower color, larger fruit, or a seedless variety. (Think seedless grapes and watermelon.) The resulting domesticated plants have genetic differences from the parent plants.

Heirloom tomatoes are valued for their taste, color, and unusual appearance.

Sun Gold tomatoes are very sweet and tolerant of cooler temperatures.

Grape tomatoes are sweet, small, and heat-tolerant.

Juliet tomatoes are sweet, small, and resistant to disease.

17. How might a cross between the Sun Gold tomato and the Juliet tomato result in a desirable hybrid?

18. A tomato breeder has noticed that a hybrid is not attracting pollinators to its flowers. What genetic change may have occurred in this hybrid? What does that mean for the long-term survival of the hybrid?

Environmental Factors Affect Plant Growth

Plant growth and survival can be affected by environmental conditions. Plants need water and nutrients to grow. Drought and poor soil conditions can severely affect a plant's health. Plants compete for the resources they need. If the area where they grow becomes overcrowded, they can die. Seasonal changes, such as unusually dry summers or late spring frosts, can disturb the life cycles of plants. Severe weather events, such as tornadoes, can destroy crops and forests.

19. Read the environmental conditions. Decide whether the condition will result in increased or decreased growth of the plant.

Cause	Effect
An unusual amount of organic matter was added to the soil.	
The habitat experienced rainfall levels well below normal for the year.	
Many seeds that fell near the parent plant germinated and began to grow.	
Tall trees grew around the plant.	

Analyze Aspen Diversity

Aspen trees are a type of tree native to cold regions. Aspens are often a pioneer species, populating areas that have recently lost vegetation to erosion, fire, or disease. They provide cover for conifer seedlings, but they often die out as the conifers take over the area. Aspens can reproduce sexually but more often reproduce asexually by sending up multiple stems from a single root system.

Aspen trees

20. Mountain aspens are often used to landscape homes in lower elevation suburban or urban areas. What factors might affect the growth of the mountain aspen in the new habitat?

_____

_____

21. Would you expect an aspen tree to be able to tolerate shade? Why or why not?

_____

_____

22. Small groves of aspen trees that appear to be separate trees may be multiple stems attached to one extensive underground root system. Would you expect individuals in a grove to be able to adapt to a change in the environment? Explain.

_____

_____

_____

_____

Continue Your Exploration

Name: _____   Date: _____

Check out the path below or go online to choose one of the other paths shown.

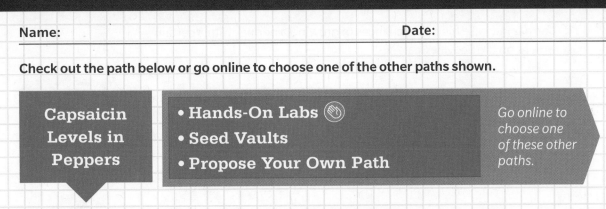

Capsaicin Levels in Peppers

- **Hands-On Labs** ✋
- **Seed Vaults**
- **Propose Your Own Path**

Go online to choose one of these other paths.

The sensation of "heat" experienced when a person eats a hot pepper is not taste. Instead the pain receptors in the mouth are triggered when a person eats a hot pepper. The Scoville Scale is a measurement scale that was created to measure the heat of a pepper, which is caused by a chemical compound called capsaicin.

The amount of capsaicin in a chili pepper is determined partially by its genetics and partially by the environmental conditions in which it grows. These conditions include factors such as temperature, humidity, soil conditions, light, and the availability of water. When chili peppers are grown in less than ideal conditions, peppers that genetically should have low heat will become hotter, while peppers that genetically should have high heat will become less hot.

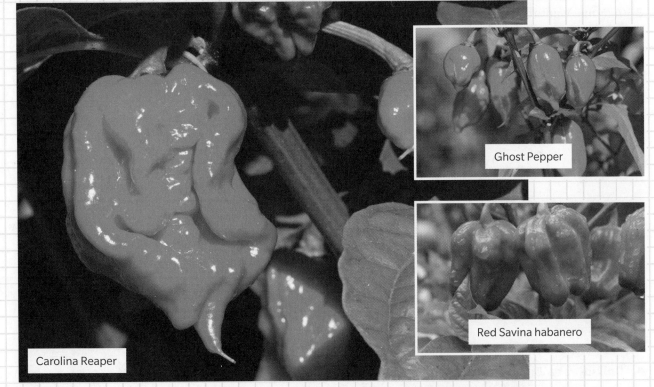

Ghost Pepper

Red Savina habanero

Carolina Reaper

The Carolina Reaper is currently the hottest chili pepper in the world, with an average measurement of 1,569,300 SHU (Scoville heat units). The Carolina Reaper is thought to be a hybrid of the Ghost Pepper and the Red Savina.

Continue Your Exploration

1. How could a farmer increase his or her chances of growing a pepper with a certain heat measurement on the Scoville Scale?

2. A chili pepper plant that produces fruit with a low heat level is grown in an area that experiences a drought. What might the farmer expect will happen to the plant? Why?

3. A farmer wants to create a chili pepper that has a higher SHU measurement than the Carolina Reaper. What could he or she do to achieve this goal?

4. **Collaborate** Brainstorm with a classmate the types of environmental stressors you could use to manipulate the heat levels in chili peppers. What conditions would you manipulate? What effects would you expect to see? Compile your ideas and create a poster or other visual presentation. Share your poster with your class.

Can You Explain It?

Name: _____   **Date:** _____

Look at the photo to revisit the sacred lotus plant.

How does the structure of the sacred lotus flower relate to reproduction?

EVIDENCE NOTEBOOK

Refer to the notes in your Evidence Notebook to help you construct an explanation for how the structure of the sacred lotus flower contributes to the reproductive success of the plant.

1. State your claim. Make sure your claim fully explains the function of the sacred lotus flower.

2. Summarize the evidence you have gathered to support your claim. Explain your reasoning.

Checkpoints

Answer the following questions to check your understanding of the lesson.

Use the photo to answer Questions 3 and 4.

3. How do you think this flower contributes to the reproductive success of the plant?

   A. The shape of the flower's petals attracts pollinators.

   B. The flower attracts bees that think they are meeting a mate.

   C. The flower scares away birds looking for a meal.

4. Number the statements in order to describe how an animal pollinator aids in the pollination of a flowering plant.

   _____ The ovules develop into seeds.

   _____ The pollinator flies to another flower, where the pollen rubs off on the flower's stigma.

   _____ The sperm within the pollen fertilizes the eggs.

   _____ The animal pollinator feeds on nectar, and the flower's pollen attaches to its body.

Use the photo to answer question 5.

5. The Cavendish banana, the banana most commonly sold in stores in North America, is under threat from a fungal infection called Fusarium wilt. The Cavendish banana is grown using asexual reproduction. Which of these factors best explains why the Cavendish banana is threatened by the fungal infection?

   A. The plants are unable to produce large numbers of offspring.

   B. The population of plants has low genetic diversity.

   C. The plants are unable to reproduce rapidly and replace plants lost to the fungus.

6. Do people who create a hybrid plant always know the exact traits that the hybrid will have? Select all that apply.

   A. Yes. People create hybrid plants because they want to combine the desirable traits of one plant with the desirable traits of another plant.

   B. No. People cannot predict every trait that a hybrid will have.

   C. No. A breeder may succeed in breeding a hybrid that has the specific trait they find desirable, but the hybrid may also have another trait that is less desirable.

Interactive Review

Complete this section to review the main concepts of the lesson.

All plants can reproduce sexually, producing genetically diverse offspring. Many can also reproduce asexually, producing genetically identical offspring.

A. How are non-flowering seed plants and flowering plants similar and different?

All plants have specialized reproductive structures. Plants can be pollinated by wind or water, and they can self-pollinate. They also rely on the help of animal pollinators.

B. Describe how animals can contribute to the reproductive success of a plant.

Both environmental and genetic factors have an effect on plant growth.

C. Draw a cause-and-effect diagram with examples of how genetic and environmental factors can affect plant growth.

Animal Reproduction and Growth

An elephant calf develops inside its mother for 20–22 months, longer than any other mammal.

By the end of this lesson . . .

you will be able to explain how an animal's behavior influences its reproductive success.

Go online to view the digital version of the Hands-On Lab for this lesson and to download additional lab resources.

CAN YOU EXPLAIN IT?

Why are these male zebras fighting?

These zebras live on the grassy plains in Etosha National Park in Namibia. Plains zebras live in family groups that include one male and several females with their offspring.

1. Think of three reasons why these zebras might be fighting with each other.

EVIDENCE NOTEBOOK As you explore the lesson, gather evidence to help you explain why male zebras fight with each other.

Describing Animal Reproduction

Scientists estimate that as many as eight or nine million species of animals may be living on Earth. Like all living things, reproduction is required for the survival of an animal species. Although some animals can reproduce asexually, sexual reproduction is the dominant type of reproduction among animals. Some individual animals may have more success in reproduction than others. What factors affect their chances of success?

These mating dragonflies reproduce sexually.

2. Write asexual reproduction, sexual reproduction, or both in the table to describe the reproductive process of each animal.

Animal	Reproductive Process	Type of Reproduction
Eastern gray squirrel (mammal)	After a male and female squirrel mate, fertilization occurs inside the female's body. She gives birth to two or more offspring that she feeds with milk from her body.	Sexual Reproduction
Roseate spoonbill (bird)	After a male and female spoonbill mate, fertilization occurs inside the female's body. The female lays eggs that will hatch into chicks.	
New Zealand mud snail (mollusk)	Female mud snails are born with genetically identical embryos inside them. They can also mate with a male to produce young snails from fertilized eggs.	
Tree frog (amphibian)	In all of the many species of tree frogs, the female lays eggs, and then the male fertilizes them.	
Walking stick (insect)	Female stick insects can produce offspring from unfertilized eggs. They can also mate with a male to produce fertilized eggs.	
Pacific salmon (fish)	Salmon eggs are laid by a female and then fertilized by a male.	

Sexual Reproduction in Animals

Sexual reproduction is a type of reproduction that involves two parents. Offspring get one copy of their genome from each parent. As a result, some organisms produced by this type of reproduction are genetically different from both parents. This genetic variation increases the chance that some offspring will have traits that may help them to survive in a changing environment.

In sexual reproduction, fertilization can be internal or external. In some species, the male and female mate, and fertilization occurs inside the female's body. In other species, the female lays eggs, and the male fertilizes them outside the female's body. Some animals lay fertilized eggs, and others give birth to live offspring.

This male damselfish is protecting the eggs he fertilized outside the female's body.

This mother robin laid eggs that will develop into young birds that she will care for.

This mother kangaroo will carry her baby (joey) in her pouch until it is fully developed.

This mother seal gave birth to her pup. She will feed it with milk from her body.

3. Sexual reproduction is the process utilized by *nearly all* / a few animals.
   To reproduce sexually, an animal *uses* / gains energy to find a mate.
   The main advantage of sexual reproduction is that it *increases* / decreases genetic variation in the population.

© Houghton Mifflin Harcourt • Image Credits: (tl) ©Luis Javier Sandoval/Oxford Scientific/Getty Images; (tr) ©vwing/iStock/Getty Images Plus/Getty Images; (br) ©Dynamic Graphics/JupiterImages/Getty Images; (bl) ©John White Photos/Moment Open/Getty Images

Asexual Reproduction in Animals

Asexual reproduction is a type of reproduction that involves only one parent. The parent passes a copy of its genes to its offspring. Unless there is a mutation, an organism produced by asexual reproduction is genetically identical to its parent and to other offspring produced asexually by the parent.

Environmental conditions can influence the type of reproduction used by an animal that can reproduce asexually or sexually. These animals might reproduce asexually when rapid reproduction is beneficial, such as the opportunity to colonize a large area. They might also reproduce asexually if conditions are unfavorable for sexual reproduction. For example, shortage of food or unsuitable temperature for survival might favor asexual reproduction.

WORD BANK
• lack of mates
• injury
• drought

4. Which environmental stimulus might result in asexual reproduction in these animals? Use the terms in the Word Bank to complete the table.

	Planaria reproduce asexually by regeneration. If the animal is split or cut into pieces, the cut segments can grow into new animals.	
	Male and female sponges can reproduce asexually by producing structures that are able to survive harsh environmental conditions.	
	Female Komodo dragons can reproduce asexually through a process that does not require fertilization of their eggs by a male.	

© Houghton Mifflin Harcourt • Image Credits: (t) ©Breck P. Kent/Animals Animals/Earth Scenes; (c) ©Paul Kay/Oxford Scientific/Getty Images; (b) ©SURZ/YAY Media AS/Alamy

 EVIDENCE NOTEBOOK

5. What type of animal is the zebra? Do you think the zebra reproduces asexually or sexually?

Language SmArts
Evaluate Reproductive Strategies

Most sea anemone species can reproduce either asexually or sexually. For example, the aggregating anemone can reproduce asexually by splitting vertically into two pieces. This process allows the animal to quickly colonize a large area.

Aggregating anemones reproduce sexually when adult animals release sperm and eggs into the water. This release can be in response to an environmental cue, such as a full moon or a low tide. The fertilized eggs that are produced when sperm and eggs unite grow into free-swimming larvae. The larvae will eventually settle to the ocean floor and establish new colonies of anemones.

aggregating anemone

6. Think about the central idea of the text above. Then circle the correct terms to complete the explanation.

   A. Anemones that colonize shallow reefs are often the result of
   asexual / sexual reproduction. They form a dense group that extends across a large, rocky area. They are hostile to genetically different animals that try to colonize the same area.

   B. Anemones that colonize new areas are often the result of
   asexual / sexual reproduction. These animals feed on plankton in open water until they find a suitable location to anchor.

Relating Animal Behaviors to Reproductive Success

Reproductive success is the ability to produce offspring that are healthy and that survive. Different species of animals use different strategies to increase their chance of reproductive success. These strategies include adult behaviors, such as courtship and parenting.

Strategies for reproductive success also include offspring behaviors. The offspring of some animal species, such as geese, imprint—or trust and follow—one or both parents. The offspring of other animals instinctively stop moving to avoid attracting the attention of predators.

These baby cardinals make loud calls and open their mouths wide.

Explore ONLINE!

7. How does the behavior of the bird's offspring contribute to reproductive success?

Courtship Behaviors

Courtship behaviors are attempts by animals to attract mates. Securing a healthy mate is one way to increase the odds of reproductive success. Courtship behaviors are exhibited mainly by males to convince females that they are worthy mates. In some species, females also engage in courtship behaviors.

Frogs, deer, bats, whales, and seals vocalize to attract a mate. Some animals, such as many species of birds, vocalize and perform dances. Males sometimes dance alone, although in some species, the female joins in.

This male manakin moonwalks across a branch to impress a mate.

The males of many bird species display brightly colored feathers or other body parts in an attempt to attract females. Most females, by contrast, have feathers of neutral colors. They are the ones being courted by the colorful males.

Male animals of some species display their strength or fight with other males to court females or to establish their "right" to a group of females. Male deer fight each other using their antlers. Male elephant seals slam their bodies into each other, while male damselflies ram each other's bodies.

The males of other animal species give presents to females or build structures for them. They do so to persuade the females to mate. Bower birds, for example, build intricate nests and show them to females, hoping to win their approval. Male kingfisher birds present females with fish.

8. What qualities do these males have that encourage females to accept them as mates? Use the Word Bank phrases to record your answers.

Male elks' antlers can weigh up to 18 kilograms (40 pounds) and stand as tall as 1.2 meters (4 feet) above their heads. Elk use their antlers to fight with other males and chase off predators.	
Male peacocks have long, beautiful tail feathers. The feathers are heavy, and the peacocks must be strong to carry them.	
These are male and female spiders. The male, which is the smaller of the two, has a gift for the female––an insect wrapped in silk.	

9. Discuss Birds sing for many reasons, but male birds produce particular songs to attract females. What other benefit might these loud vocalizations provide to the male? Talk about your ideas with a partner.

 EVIDENCE NOTEBOOK

10. Is the fighting behavior of the zebras from the beginning of the lesson a courtship or a parenting behavior? How might this behavior affect the reproductive success of zebras? Record your evidence.

Parenting Behaviors

Parenting behaviors are attempts by animals to ensure their offspring's survival. These behaviors are another way that animals increase their odds of reproductive success.

Many species of animals build nests for their eggs and young. Males or females, or both, gather the materials and construct the nests. One or both parents might guard eggs and offspring in the nest.

Animals feed their young in a variety of ways. Female mammals nurse their young with milk from their bodies. Other species gather or hunt food for their offspring. Sometimes animals, such as some species of birds, eat food and then regurgitate it for their young. The offspring are better able to eat the food once it has been partially broken down by the parent bird's digestive system.

Animals care for their young for varying lengths of time. Many reptiles abandon their eggs before they hatch, so the young are on their own. Other species stay with their offspring for a few months (birds) or for years (elephants). Some animals also teach offspring how to fend for themselves. For example, lions teach their young to hunt.

Some animals sacrifice their health or their lives for their offspring. A male emperor penguin holds a single egg on the top of his feet, covered with a layer of skin to keep it warm. He does this for 60–68 days through extremely cold and windy conditions, with no access to food. Another example of parent sacrifice is the female of many octopus species that guard and care for their eggs for months—even years—before they hatch. After the eggs hatch, the female dies. After the eggs of the killdeer bird hatch, both parents keep predators away from their offspring by pretending to be injured. A killdeer will drag its "broken wing" along the ground, luring the predators away from the young birds. Adult killdeers sometimes are caught and killed by predators while employing this strategy.

> **WORD BANK**
> - nest building
> - defending offspring
> - feeding offspring
> - teaching offspring

11. What parental behavior is shown by each of these animals?

red squirrel

Bengal tiger and cubs

penguins and caracara

brown bear and cubs

Do the Math

Analyze Female Mate Choice

guppy

Guppies are freshwater tropical fish native to South America. Males are usually brightly colored, which makes them popular aquarium fish. Some scientists investigate the characteristics that female guppies prefer when choosing mates. These bar graphs show the results of experiments that tested female preference for three different tail sizes.

Analyze the data in the graph and use it to answer the questions below.

12. Use the data from the graph to describe the three experiments in your own words.

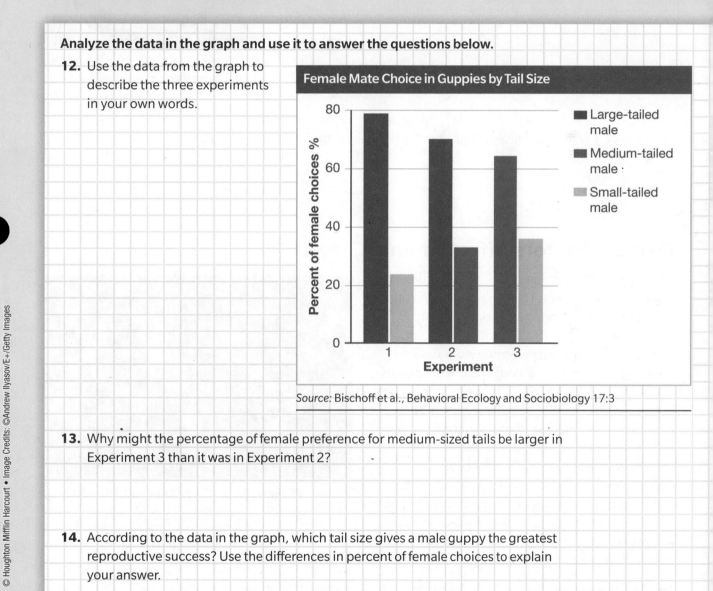

Female Mate Choice in Guppies by Tail Size

- Large-tailed male
- Medium-tailed male
- Small-tailed male

Source: Bischoff et al., Behavioral Ecology and Sociobiology 17:3

13. Why might the percentage of female preference for medium-sized tails be larger in Experiment 3 than it was in Experiment 2?

14. According to the data in the graph, which tail size gives a male guppy the greatest reproductive success? Use the differences in percent of female choices to explain your answer.

© Houghton Mifflin Harcourt • Image Credits: ©Andrew Ilyasov/E+/Getty Images

Explaining Factors That Influence Animal Growth

To live and grow, animals need five basic environmental resources: space, shelter, food, water, and oxygen. If any of these resources change, the growth and development of the animals dependent on them will also change. If the changes are large enough, the animals' growth and health will be affected.

Common goldfish will eat as much food as they are given and produce large amounts of waste.

15. Aquarium recommendations for a common goldfish are at least 20 gallons of water. Do you think the bowl shown here meets the recommended requirement for maintaining a healthy goldfish? Why or why not?

16. How do you think the growth of the goldfish is affected by the bowl conditions?

Genetic Factors Affect Animal Growth

Offspring of sexually reproducing parents inherit one allele from each parent. Therefore, the combination of alleles that an offspring inherits is different from the combination of alleles of either parent. Differences in traits can give some individuals an advantage over other individuals. Some offspring might have better eyesight or hearing, stronger jaws or teeth, or thicker fur than other offspring. Some might not have inherited diseases that others have.

The gray wolf shares a common ancestor with modern dog breeds.

These genetic differences affect not only individual offspring. They also affect entire populations . Due to differences in genetic traits, some individuals in an animal population might be able to survive changing environmental conditions better than other individuals. As a result, the population can continue to exist in the community.

17. The narrow chest, long legs, and large paws of wolves allow them to run at very high speeds. How might these traits contribute to the growth of the wolf?

   A. They enable the wolf to find mates.

   B. They make the wolf an excellent parent.

   C. They enable the wolf to chase and catch prey.

   D. They allow the wolf to communicate with other wolves.

Engineer It
Explain Trait Selection in Dog Breeds

At least 12,000 years ago, humans began to domesticate members of a wolf-like species. Scientists think that this animal is a common ancestor shared both by the gray wolf and the dogs of today's world.

When you compare the traits of the various dog breeds with wolves, many differences—and a few similarities—emerge. In general, domestic dogs have thinner coats, shorter legs, smaller paws, and smaller teeth than their wolf relatives. Dogs share some behaviors with wolves, such as putting their ears back to show submission.

Each of the more than 300 different dog breeds was developed over a long period of time. Humans selected the dogs with the traits they wanted and then bred them. For example, the poodle was developed as a water retriever of fallen birds for hunters. Its keen intelligence, webbed feet, and curly coat that is almost waterproof make it well suited to hunt in rivers and marshes. These traits are very different from the traits of the wolf-like ancestor of long ago.

The greyhound was bred as a hunting dog. It chases and captures prey, such as rabbits.

The dachshund was also bred as a hunting dog. It captures rats and other small animals that burrow in the ground.

18. How might a breeder select for dogs with longer legs?

19. **Discuss** Look at the body types of each of the breeds above. Discuss how the body features of each dog relate to the function that the dog was bred to perform.

Environmental Factors Affect Animal Growth

Genetics is not the only factor that affects animal growth. The conditions of an animal's environment also affect growth and development. Beneficial environmental conditions include abundant food, water, air, and space. They also include a habitat free from pollution, as well as sufficient shelter from predators.

Harmful environmental conditions include weather, such as drought, that deprives animals of water or that negatively impacts the growth of the plants that the animals eat. Other harmful environmental conditions are overcrowding, pollution, and habitat destruction.

The blackbuck antelope is an herbivore native to India and Pakistan.

20. Read the condition and decide if it will result in the decreased growth or increased growth of the blackbuck antelope.

Causes	Effects
A disease has infected a plant in the blackbuck's diet.	
Good weather conditions have resulted in the increased growth of a plant in the blackbuck's diet.	
Drought has caused a decrease of the plant species the blackbuck eats in its habitat.	
Human development has caused a decrease in the blackbuck habitat.	
Humans have begun hunting the blackbuck antelope.	
Regular rains have resulted in a larger-than-average water supply.	

Hands-On Lab
Model the Growth of an Animal

You will work with a group to design a board game that models how genetic and environmental factors affect animals. Then you will create the board game with provided materials. Finally, you will switch games with another group, play the other group's game, and give the group feedback about the game.

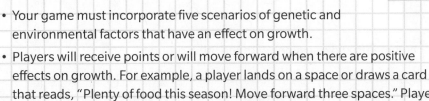

Procedure

STEP 1 With your group, brainstorm an idea for a board game that models the growth of an animal over time. The game must also meet the following conditions:

- Your game must incorporate five scenarios of genetic and environmental factors that have an effect on growth.

- Players will receive points or will move forward when there are positive effects on growth. For example, a player lands on a space or draws a card that reads, "Plenty of food this season! Move forward three spaces." Players will move backward or will lose a turn when there are negative effects on growth. For example, a player lands on a space or draws a card that reads, "Drought in progress! Lose a turn."

STEP 2 Once your group has finished brainstorming, discuss with group members the details of your game. Record your scenarios.

STEP 3 After your group has worked out all the details, create the game using the provided materials.

Analysis

STEP 4 Trade games with another group. Play the other group's game. As you play, write your comments and questions about the game: What did you like about the game? Is there anything the other group could do to improve its depiction of the genetic and environmental factors that influence the growth of animals?

STEP 5 Exchange your comments and questions with the other group.

STEP 6 Review the other group's comments and questions about your group's game. What could your group do to improve the game so that it better depicts how genetic and environmental factors influence the growth of animals?

Distinguish Between Genetic and Environmental Factors

A rancher is raising Angus cattle in Colorado. The rancher notices that when he moves his cattle from a lower elevation to a higher elevation, some cattle grow more than others.

- Cattle that grew more after the move also grew more between the time they stopped drinking milk from their mothers and the time they reached one year of age.

- Cattle that did not grow as much after the move also did not grow as much between the time they stopped drinking milk and the time they reached one year of age.

Angus cattle are mammals that reproduce sexually.

21. Angus cattle that grow more at higher altitudes might withstand that environmental change better than other cattle because there is a (an) *genetic / environmental* factor that helps them survive better in a changing environment. The factor is somehow related to the fact that the cattle grew *more / less* than others did between weaning age and yearling age.

Continue Your Exploration

Name: _____   Date: _____

Check out the path below or go online to choose one of the other paths shown.

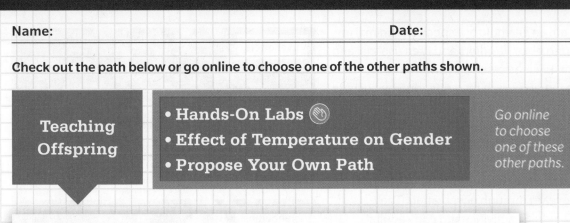

Teaching Offspring

- **Hands-On Labs** 👋
- **Effect of Temperature on Gender**
- **Propose Your Own Path**

Go online to choose one of these other paths.

One way adult animals try to ensure their reproductive success is through parenting behaviors. Parents teach their offspring in a variety of ways. Some parents directly teach skills or train offspring gradually over time. In other species of animals, offspring may simply observe adults and then use trial and error to learn.

Meerkats are prairie dog-like mammals that thrive in large packs. They use direct teaching of skills as a parenting behavior. Parents teach their offspring how to capture and kill dangerous prey, such as scorpions. They bring nearly dead animals to the offspring because the prey is too dangerous to start with for instructional purposes. They might render the prey animals harmless, for instance, by removing the stinger. This teaching behavior is not limited to the actual parents. Other adult meerkats, called helpers, will also teach offspring that are not theirs.

1. What benefit might adult meerkats gain by helping others' offspring learn how to capture and kill dangerous prey?

meerkats

Continue Your Exploration

River otters are an example of a species of animal in which offspring observe adults and then use trial and error to learn. River otters do not know how to swim at birth. The females teach their offspring by pushing them into the water when the offspring are about two months old. The females will carry the offspring on their backs if help is needed. The offspring learn by doing.

river otters

Orangutans are another species in which the offspring learn through observation. They participate in adults' activities and copy adults' behavior. Offspring remain with their mothers for eight years or more. They learn everything from how to swing through trees to how to find food to how to build a nest for sleeping in at night.

orangutans

2. For adult animals, what are the advantages of making the investment of time and resources to teach offspring life skills?

3. For adult animals, what are the disadvantages of making the investment of time and resources to teach offspring life skills?

4. **Collaborate** Brainstorm with a classmate how human offspring learn from their parents. What do you think you learned from your parents simply by observing and copying them? What did you learn by trying to help your parents with activities? What did your parents directly teach you? Compile your ideas and create a poster or other visual method of displaying them. Share your poster with your class.

Can You Explain It?

Name: _____   **Date:** _____

Look at the photo to revisit the behavior of male zebras.

Why are these male zebras fighting?

 EVIDENCE NOTEBOOK
Refer to the notes in your Evidence Notebook to help you construct an explanation for why the male zebras are fighting.

1. State your claim. Make sure your claim fully explains the function of the behavior.

2. Summarize the evidence you have gathered to support your claim and explain your reasoning.

Checkpoints

Answer the following questions to check your understanding of the lesson.

Use the photo to answer Questions 3 and 4.

3. This male midwife toad most likely reproduces asexually / sexually.

This male midwife toad will carry the eggs he fertilized on his back until they are ready to hatch.

4. How does this behavior contribute to the toad's reproductive success?

   A. He is ensuring that his genes are passed on to surviving offspring.

   B. He cannot mate with other females while he is carrying the eggs.

   C. He will be more attractive to females in the future.

Use the photo to answer Questions 5 and 6.

5. The type of behavior shown in this photo is best described as offspring / courtship / parenting behavior.

6. What is the function of the behavior shown in the photo? Select all that apply.

   A. The offspring has a better chance of survival if it is clean and free of parasites.

   B. The mother's reproductive success is improved if the offspring does not die due to disease or infection.

   C. The father's reproductive success is improved if the offspring does not die due to disease or infection.

Interactive Review

Complete this section to review the main concepts of the lesson.

Sexual reproduction is the dominant type of reproduction among animals, although some also reproduce asexually.

A. Why is sexual reproduction the dominant type of reproduction among animals?

Courtship, parenting, and offspring behaviors contribute to the reproductive success of animals.

B. Describe one courtship behavior and one parenting behavior, including how each behavior contributes to the reproductive success of an animal.

Genetic and environmental factors influence the growth of animals.

C. Explain the causes and effects that illustrate how different factors can influence growth.

© Houghton Mifflin Harcourt • Image Credits: (t) ©Milan Vachal/Shutterstock; (c) ©Shawn Hempel/Shutterstock; (b) ©Sylvain Cordier/Photographer's Choice/Getty Images

Choose one of the activities to explore how this unit connects to other topics.

☐ Earth Science Connection

Climate and Reproduction Patterns in reproduction and growth relate to patterns in biome distribution on Earth. While organisms at the equator might reproduce year round, organisms at the frigid poles must often focus more on basic survival needs, leaving little time or energy for growth and reproduction.

Research the climate of two terrestrial biomes. Compare and contrast patterns of reproduction and growth for two organisms, one from each biome. Create a multimedia presentation to share what you learn with the class.

☐ Art Connection

Landscape Architects Landscape architects use plant knowledge to make outdoor spaces beautiful and functional. They carefully choose plants with a variety of reproductive strategies that can be successful in the local environment during different seasons. For example, landscape architects for an amusement park might arrange plants according to flowering season to ensure vibrant blooms all year long.

Research different plants and design a landscape for an outdoor space in your community. Choose at least five climate-appropriate plants that use a variety of reproductive strategies. Explain the practical and artistic purposes for each plant in a landscape diagram you share with the class.

Butchart Gardens in British Columbia, Canada

☐ Computer Science Connection

DNA Databases Geneticists produce profiles for individuals using DNA. Scientists use DNA databases to store thousands of profiles to make predictions based on genetic patterns they observe in populations. For example, scientists use DNA data to predict which groups of people are most likely to have a genetic disease.

Research DNA databases maintained by the government, a university, or a private company. Evaluate how these databases are used. Then analyze the pros and cons to determine if the benefits outweigh the risks associated with DNA tracking. Prepare a brief presentation to share with the class.

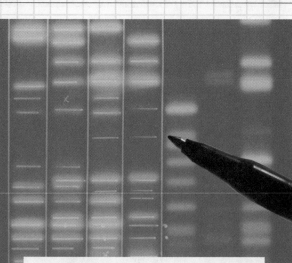

Comparing DNA "fingerprints" of four people

Name: _____   Date: _____

Complete this review to check your understanding of the unit.

Use the chart to answer Questions 1–3.

1. Blood type inheritance involves three alleles, which are shown in the chart as A, B, and O. Study the genotypes and resulting blood types of Sam and Heidi's children. Based on this information, which statement about the alleles for blood type is correct?

   A. O is dominant over A and B.

   B. A and B are each dominant over O.

   C. Only A is dominant over O.

   D. A, B, and O alleles are equally dominant.

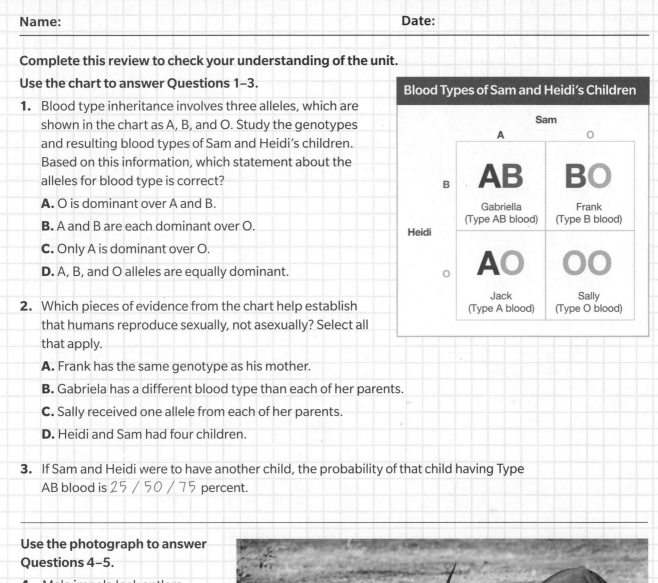

Blood Types of Sam and Heidi's Children

	Sam	
	A	O
B	**AB** Gabriella (Type AB blood)	**BO** Frank (Type B blood)
Heidi O	**AO** Jack (Type A blood)	**OO** Sally (Type O blood)

2. Which pieces of evidence from the chart help establish that humans reproduce sexually, not asexually? Select all that apply.

   A. Frank has the same genotype as his mother.

   B. Gabriela has a different blood type than each of her parents.

   C. Sally received one allele from each of her parents.

   D. Heidi and Sam had four children.

3. If Sam and Heidi were to have another child, the probability of that child having Type AB blood is 25 / 50 / 75 percent.

Use the photograph to answer Questions 4–5.

4. Male impala lock antlers to compete for mates. The physical advantages that one male has over the other depend on:

   A. genetic factors.

   B. environmental factors.

   C. both genetic and environmental factors.

5. Why is the winning male impala likely to have more reproductive success? Select all that apply.

   A. They are healthier and likely to produce healthy, viable gametes.

   B. They will attract more mates.

   C. They have only beneficial genes.

   D. They will defend the female and offspring more effectively than a weaker male.

Name: **Date:**

6. Think of an example or strategy related to each category of reproduction listed in the table. Describe the structure-function relationship for each of your examples, and then describe each in terms of cause and effect on successful reproduction.

Reproduction Category	Structure and Function	Cause and Effect
Asexual reproduction in plants		
Sexual reproduction in plants		
Asexual reproduction in animals		
Sexual reproduction in animals		

Use the diagram about reproduction in pine trees to answer Questions 7–10.

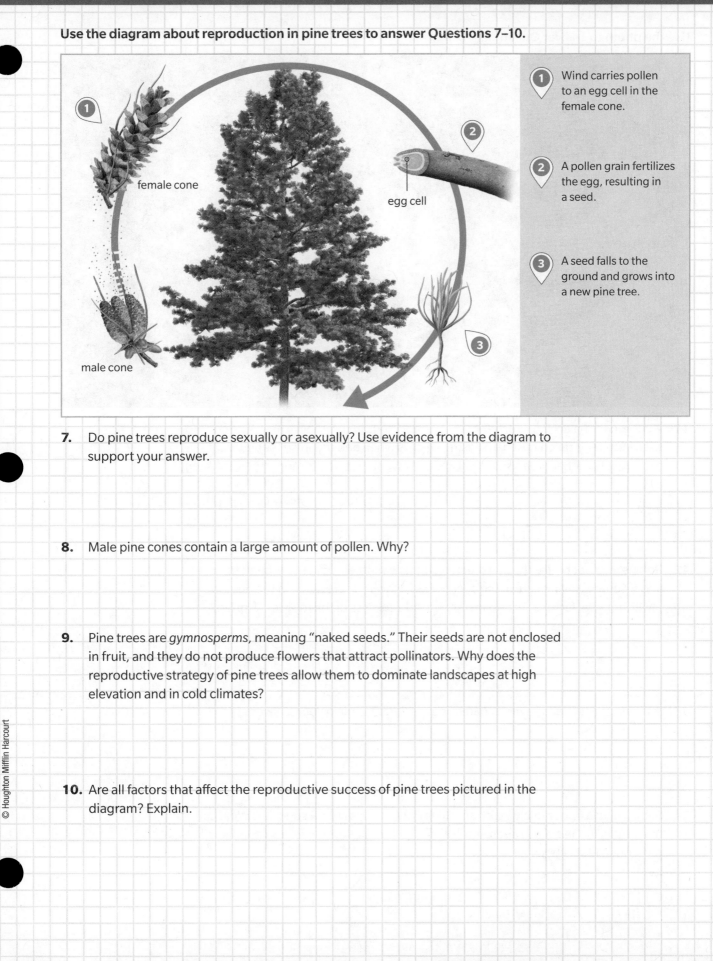

female cone

egg cell

male cone

1. Wind carries pollen to an egg cell in the female cone.

2. A pollen grain fertilizes the egg, resulting in a seed.

3. A seed falls to the ground and grows into a new pine tree.

7. Do pine trees reproduce sexually or asexually? Use evidence from the diagram to support your answer.

8. Male pine cones contain a large amount of pollen. Why?

9. Pine trees are *gymnosperms,* meaning "naked seeds." Their seeds are not enclosed in fruit, and they do not produce flowers that attract pollinators. Why does the reproductive strategy of pine trees allow them to dominate landscapes at high elevation and in cold climates?

10. Are all factors that affect the reproductive success of pine trees pictured in the diagram? Explain.

Use the photo to answer Questions 11–14.

11. A cuckoo bird placed one of her gray-speckled eggs in this robin's nest. The cuckoo uses a strategy called nest parasitism, which is when one organism benefits at the expense of another organism. What are the advantages of this reproductive strategy?

12. Robins may not notice the unexpected egg. The mother robin may spend time and resources taking care of the cuckoo bird. How is its presence in the nest an environmental factor affecting the growth and success of the robin's offspring?

13. Is taking care of eggs a type of parenting behavior? Explain your answer.

14. Some cuckoo eggs are blue with speckles instead of gray with speckles. What causes this variety in the cuckoo eggs and how might it improve the cuckoo's chance of reproductive success?

Name: _____ Date: _____

Save the Whitebark Pines!

The stately whitebark pines of Yellowstone National Park are in trouble! Normally, cold temperatures at the tree line keep pine beetles, which infect the trees, away. However, the cold temperature band has shrunk with recent climate change, leaving more trees at risk of pine beetle infection. A fungus also infects the trees, though scientists are encouraged to see that some pines have an inherited resistance to the fungus. The pines are important to many species in Yellowstone, including other coniferous trees, pine squirrels, birds, and grizzly bears.

As part of an Eco-Task Force, you will develop a plan to increase the number of healthy whitebark pines in Yellowstone. You should consider genetic solutions, as well as actions that might improve reproductive success and enhance sapling growth. Save the whitebark pines!

Clark's nutcracker on a healthy whitebark pine

Whitebark pine infected with fungus that causes blister rust

The steps below will help guide your research and develop your recommendation.

1. **Define the Problem** With your team, write a statement defining the problem you have been asked to solve. What factors limit the success of the pines?

2. **Conduct Research** Using library or Internet resources, learn more about how environmental scientists help threatened populations. What can your Eco-Task Force do to improve the genetic variation, growth, and reproduction of the whitebark pines in Yellowstone?

3. **Develop a Model** Genetic solutions often require breeding programs. Use Punnett squares to show how you could increase fungus resistance in whitebark populations, depending on whether the allele for resistance is recessive or dominant. Show what crosses would be ideal in each situation. What process will the Eco-Task Force need to use to breed fungus-resistant offspring?

4. **Recommend a Solution** Make a recommendation based on your research. How will your team protect adult trees from pine beetles and fungus, as well as ensure successful growth of new saplings?

5. **Communicate** How will you convince officials that your plan will work? Create a multimedia presentation to present your plan to save the whitebark pines in Yellowstone. Use evidence and reasoning to support your claims.

✓ Self-Check

	I listed all factors (genetic, reproductive, and environmental) that limit the number of whitebark pines in Yellowstone.
	I researched how environmental scientists help threatened populations.
	I used a model to consider genetic solutions that could help the whitebark pines.
	My solutions are based on research and a correct understanding of the pines' pattern of growth and reproduction.
	My presentation used effective scientific argumentation to defend the Eco-Task Force proposal.

Glossary

Pronunciation Key							
Sound	**Symbol**	**Example**	**Respelling**	**Sound**	**Symbol**	**Example**	**Respelling**
ă	a	pat	PAT	ŏ	ah	bottle	BAHT'l
ā	ay	pay	PAY	ō	oh	toe	TOH
âr	air	care	KAIR	ô	aw	caught	KAWT
ä	ah	father	FAH•ther	ôr	ohr	roar	ROHR
är	ar	argue	AR•gyoo	oi	oy	noisy	NOYZ•ee
ch	ch	chase	CHAYS	o͞o	u	book	BUK
ĕ	e	pet	PET	o͞o	oo	boot	BOOT
ĕ (at end of a syllable)	eh	settee lessee	seh•TEE leh•SEE	ou	ow	pound	POWND
ĕr	ehr	merry	MEHR•ee	s	s	center	SEN•ter
ē	ee	beach	BEECH	sh	sh	cache	CASH
g	g	gas	GAS	ŭ	uh	flood	FLUHD
ĭ	i	pit	PIT	ûr	er	bird	BERD
ĭ (at end of a syllable)	ih	guitar	gih•TAR	z	z	xylophone	ZY•luh•fohn
ī	y eye (only for a complete syllable)	pie island	PY EYE•luhnd	z	z	bags	BAGZ
îr	ir	hear	HIR	zh	zh	decision	dih•SIZH•uhn
j	j	germ	JERM	ə	uh	around broken focus	uh•ROWND BROH•kuhn FOH•kuhs
k	k	kick	KIK	ər	er	winner	WIN•er
ng	ng	thing	THING	th	th	thin they	THIN THAY
ngk	ngk	bank	BANGK	w	w	one	WUHN
				wh	hw	whether	HWETH•er

asexual reproduction (ay•SEK•shoo•uhl ree•pruh•DUHK•shuhn)
reproduction that does not involve the union of sex cells and in which one parent produces offspring that are genetically identical to the parent (143)
reproducción asexual   reproducción que no involucra la unión de células sexuales, en la que un solo progenitor produce descendencia que es genéticamente igual al progenitor

behavior (bih•HAYV•yer)
an action that an individual carries out in response to a stimulus or to the environment (105)
conducta   una acción que un individuo realiza en respuesta a un estímulo o a su ambiente

cell (SEL)
in biology, the smallest unit that can perform all life processes; cells are covered by a membrane and contain DNA and cytoplasm (6)
célula   en biología, la unidad más pequeña que puede realizar todos los procesos vitales; las células están cubiertas por una membrana y tienen ADN y citoplasma

cell membrane (SEL MEM•brayn)
a phospholipid layer that covers a cell's surface and acts as a barrier between the inside of a cell and the cell's environment (20)
membrana celular   una capa de fosfolípidos que cubre la superficie de la célula y funciona como una barrera entre el interior de la célula y el ambiente de la célula

cell wall (SEL WAWL)
a rigid structure that surrounds the cell membrane and provides support to the cell (21)
pared celular   una estructura rígida que rodea la membrana celular y le brinda soporte a la célula

chloroplast (KLOHR•uh•plast)
an organelle found in plant and algae cells where photosynthesis occurs (21)
cloroplasto   un organelo que se encuentra en las células vegetales y en las células de las algas, en el cual se lleva a cabo la fotosíntesis

chromosome (KROH•muh•sohm)
in a eukaryotic cell, one of the structures in the nucleus that are made up of DNA and protein; in a prokaryotic cell, the main ring of DNA (128)
cromosoma   en una célula eucariótica, una de las estructuras del núcleo que está hecha de ADN y proteína; en una célula procariótica, el anillo principal de ADN

circulatory system (SER•kyuh•luh•tohr•ee SIS•tuhm)
the body system made up of the heart, of the blood vessels, and of the blood (85)
sistema circulatorio   sistema del cuerpo formado por el corazón, los vasos sanguíneos y la sangre

digestive system (dy•JES•tiv SIS•tuhm)
the organs that break down food so that it can be used by the body (84)
aparato digestivo   los órganos que descomponen la comida de modo que el cuerpo la pueda usar

excretory system (EK•skrih•tohr•ee SIS•tuhm)
the system that collects and excretes nitrogenous wastes and excess water from the body in the form of urine (84)
aparato excretor   el sistema que recolecta y elimina del cuerpo los desperdicios nitrogenados y el exceso de agua en forma de orina

gamete (GAM•eet)
a haploid reproductive cell that unites with another haploid reproductive cell to form a zygote (147)
gameto   una célula reproductiva haploide que se une con otra célula reproductiva haploide para formar un cigoto

gene (JEEN)
one set of instructions for an inherited trait (128)
gene   un conjunto de instrucciones para un carácter heredado

heredity (huh•RED•ih•tee)
the passing of genetic traits from parent to offspring (128)
herencia   la transmisión de caracteres genéticos de padres a hijos

homeostasis (hoh•mee•oh•STAY•sis)
the maintenance of a constant internal state in a changing environment (100)
homeostasis   la capacidad de mantener un estado interno constante en un ambiente en cambio

inheritance (in•HEHR•ih•tuhns)
the process by which a characteristic is passed from parent to offspring (126)
herencia   proceso por el cual una característica se pasa de los progenitores a sus crías

leaf (LEEF)
a plant organ that is the main site of photosynthesis and transpiration (69)
hoja   órgano de la planta que es el lugar principal de fotosíntesis y transpiración

memory (MEM•uh•ree)
the ability to store and recall past experience (106)
memoria habilidad para almacenar y recordar experiencias pasadas

mitochondrion (my•toh•KAHN•dree•uhn)
in eukaryotic cells, the organelle that is the site of cellular respiration, which releases energy for use by the cell (21)
mitocondria en las células eucarióticas, el organelo donde se lleva a cabo la respiración celular, la cual libera energía para que utilice la célula

multicellular organism (muhl•tee•SEL•yuh•luhr OHR•guh•niz•uhm)
an organism that consists of more than one cell (8)
organismo multicelular organismo conformado por más de una célula

muscular system (MUS•kyuh•ler SIS•tuhm)
the organ system whose primary function is movement and flexibility (86)
sistema muscular el sistema de órganos cuya función principal es permitir el movimiento y la flexibilidad

nervous system (NER•vuhs SIS•tuhm)
the structures that control the actions and reactions of the body in response to stimuli from the environment; it is formed by billions of specialized nerve cells called neurons (86)
sistema nervioso las estructuras que controlan las acciones y reacciones del cuerpo en respuesta a los estímulos del ambiente; está formado por miles de millones de células nerviosas especializadas llamadas neuronas

nucleus (NOO•klee•uhs)
in a eukaryotic cell, a membrane-bound organelle that contains the cell's DNA and that has a role in processes such as growth, metabolism, and reproduction (21)
núcleo en una célula eucariótica, un organelo cubierto por una membrana, el cual contiene el ADN de la célula y participa en procesos tales como el crecimiento, metabolismo y reproducción

offspring (AWF•spring)
a new organism that results from sexual or asexual reproduction (142)
descendencia nuevo organismo que resulta de la reproducción sexual o asexual

organ (OHR•guhn)
a collection of tissues that carry out a specialized function of the body (50)
órgano un conjunto de tejidos que desempeñan una función especializada en el cuerpo

organelle (ohr•guhn•EL)
one of the small bodies that are found in the cytoplasm of a cell and that are specialized to perform a specific function (20)
organelo uno de los cuerpos pequeños que se encuentran en el citoplasma de una célula y que están especializados para llevar a cabo una función específica

organism (OHR•guh•niz•uhm)
a living thing; anything that can carry out life processes independently (6, 48)
organismo un ser vivo; cualquier cosa que pueda llevar a cabo procesos vitales independientemente

organ system (OHR•guhn SIS•tuhm)
a group of organs that work together to perform body functions (50)
aparato (o sistema) de órganos un grupo de órganos que trabajan en conjunto para desempeñar funciones corporales

pollination (pahl•uh•NAY•shuhn)
the transfer of pollen from the male reproductive structures to the female structures of seed plants (160)
polinización la transferencia de polen de las estructuras reproductoras masculinas a las estructuras femeninas de las plantas con semillas

protein (PROH•teen)
a molecule that is made up of amino acids and that is needed to build and repair body structures and to regulate processes in the body (128)
proteína una molécula formada por aminoácidos que es necesaria para construir y reparar estructuras corporales y para regular procesos del cuerpo

respiratory system (RES•per•uh•tohr•ee SIS•tuhm)
a collection of organs whose primary function is to take in oxygen and expel carbon dioxide; the organs of this system include the lungs, the throat, and the passageways that lead to the lungs (85)
aparato respiratorio un conjunto de órganos cuya función principal es tomar oxígeno y expulsar dióxido de carbono; los órganos de este aparato incluyen a los pulmones, la garganta y las vías que llevan a los pulmones

root (ROOT)
the mainly underground organ of vascular plants that holds plants in place and absorbs and stores water and minerals from the soil (70)
raíz el órgano principalmente subterráneo de las plantas vasculares, el cual mantiene a las plantas en su lugar y absorbe y almacena agua y minerales del suelo

S–Z

seed (SEED)
a plant embryo that is enclosed in a protective coat (160)
semilla el embrión de una planta que está encerrado en una cubierta protectora

sensory receptor (SEN•suh•ree rih•SEP•tuhr)
a specialized structure that contains the ends of sensory neurons and that responds to specific types of stimuli (101)
receptor sensorial una estructura especializada que contiene los extremos de las neuronas sensoriales y que responde a tipos específicos de estímulos

sexual reproduction (SEK•shoo•uhl ree•pruh•DUHK•shuhn)
reproduction in which the sex cells from two parents unite to produce offspring that share traits from both parents (143)
reproducción sexual reproducción en la que se unen las células sexuales de los dos progenitores para producir descendencia que comparte caracteres de ambos progenitores

stem (STEM)
a plant structure that provides support and transports nutrients (70)
tallo estructura de la planta que le provee soporte y que transporta nutrientes

tissue (TISH•oo)
a group of similar cells that perform a common function (50)
tejido un grupo de células similares que llevan a cabo una función común

trait (TRAYT)
a genetically determined characteristic (50,126)
carácter una característica determinada genéticamente

unicellular organism (yoo•nih•SEL•yuh•luhr OHR•guh•niz•uhm)
an organism that consists of a single cell (8)
organismo unicelular organismo conformado por solo una célula

Index

Page numbers for key terms are in **boldface** type.
Page numbers in *italic* type indicate illustrative material, such as photographs, graphs, charts and maps.

A

acquired trait, 132, 139
adenine (A), 135
adrenal gland, *119*
African cichlid fish, 124, *124*
aggregating anemone, 181, *181*
air sac, *55*
algal, 18, *18*
allele, 128, 130, 132, *132*, 133, 134, 139, 148–150, 186, 197
Ameiva lizard, 98, *98*
amphibian, 83, 94, 145, *145*, *155*, 178
analysis
 of animal body system interactions, 87, 88–92
 of aspen diversity, 170
 of Hands-On Lab results, 11, 26, 51, 71, 91, 107, 131, 148, 166, 190
 structure and function of bird bones, 55, *55*
 of system responses, 120
Angus cattle, 190, *190*
animal
 asexual reproduction of, 143, 178, 180, *180*
 courtship behaviors, 182–183
 diversity of, 83, *83*
 factors influencing growth, 186, 188
 hibernation of, 106, *106*
 information processing in, 98–110
 migration of, 56, *56*, *109*, 109–110
 as multicellular organisms, 8
 needs of, 186, 188
 parenting behaviors, 184, *184*, 191, 191–192, *192*, *194*, *195*
 pollination by, 163, *164*, 175
 reproduction of, 142, 143, 179
 reproductive success of, 182–185
 response to information, 86, 89, 92, 100–106
 seed dispersal by, 160, 163–164, 166

sexual reproduction of, 178–179, *195*
 structure and function of tissues of, 53, *53*
animal body
 comparing systems, 82–87
 functions of, 84–87
 system interactions, 88–89
 as systems, 80–94
animal cell, 22, *22*, 24
Annelida phylum, 83, *83*
antennae, 86, 102
anther, *164*, 165
Appaloosa horses, 141, *141*, 153
Arctic tern, 110, *110*
Art Connection
 The Golden Ratio and the Fibonacci Sequence, 114
 Landscape Architects, 196
 Making Art of the Invisible World, 36
arthropod, 83, *83*
Arthropoda phylum, 83, *83*
asexual reproduction, 143
 of animals, 178, 180, *181*
 of aspen trees, 170
 of fungi, 152
 genetic material passed in, 132, 145, *145*
 offspring of, 155, *155*
 of plants, 152, 162, *162*, 175
 sexual reproduction compared to, 150
aspen tree, 170, *170*, 175
Assessment
 Lesson Self-Check, 15–17, 33–35, 61–63, 77–79, 95–97, 111–113, 137–139, 153–155, 173–175, 193–195
 Unit Performance Task, 41–42, 119–120, 201–202
 Unit Review, 37–41, 115–118

B

bacteria, *24*
 asexual reproduction of, 143, *143*
 in eukaryotic cells, 31
 generation time, 146
 as prokaryotes, 21, *21*, *23*, *24*, 145
 as unicellular organisms, 8
bar graph, 185, *185*
bark, *118*
barrel sponge, 83, *83*
bases of DNA, 129, *129*, 135, *135*
bat, 102, *102*, 121, 163, *164*, 182
beak of nautilus, 81, 88, 95
bee
 colony collapse disorder, 167
 as pollinators, 143
 reproduction, 151
behavior, 105
 breaching of whales, 89, *89*
 courtship behavior, 182–183, 185
 of dogs, 187
 hibernation, 106, *106*
 imprinting, 182
 influence on reproductive success, 182–183
 innate behavior, 105, 117
 learned behavior, 105, *105*, 106
 migration, 56, *56*, *109*, 109–110
 parenting behavior, 184, *191*, 191–192, *192*
 response to environment/stimulus, 43, *43*, 98, 100, 102–103, 105, *105*, 113, *113*
 study of, 93–94
 of zebras, 177, *177*, 193, *193*
Bengal tiger, 184, *184*
bigfin reef squid, 83, *83*
bilateral symmetry, 83
binary fission, *143*
biologist, 31–32
biome, 196
biomimetic lens, 60, *60*

© Houghton Mifflin Harcourt

© Houghton Mifflin Harcourt

P–Q

© Houghton Mifflin Harcourt

organ systems of animals, 82–87

plant bodies as, 64–76

predicting effect of failure, 92

respiratory system, 55, *55*, 57, *57*, **85**

responsible for water balance, *119*, 119–120

structure and function of plant body systems, 69–70

system feedback, 101, *101*

systems analysis, 45

T

tables

of animal responses to needs, *56*

of behavior and memory in animals, *105*

of careers in science, 12

of cause and effect, 170, *188*

of cause-and-effect relationships in the body, *116*

comparing transport systems, *71*

creating graphs from, *146*

of data, *107*, 148, 149, *188*

of differences in cells, *24*

of genotype and phenotypes, *134*

of living and nonliving things, *8*

of observations, *7, 11*

of parts of cells, *38*

of processes of systems, *88*

of questions, 2, 44, 122

of reproduction strategies, 198

of reproductive strategies, *198*

of responses to environment, *89, 91*

of seed dispersal methods, *161*

of similarities and differences of plants, *66*

of structure and function of plant organs, *54*

of surface area–to-volume ratios, *26*

of types of reproduction in animals, *178*

of types of reproduction in plants, *162*

of types of stimuli, *102*

Why It Matters, 2, 44, 122

tadpole, 142, *142, 155*

Take It Further

Biomimicry, 59–60

Capsaicin Levels in Peppers, 171–172

Careers in Science: Animal Scientists, 93–94

Factors That Influence Reproduction, 151–152

Growing Plants in Space, *75,* 75–76

Microscopes over Time, 13–14

Migration, 109–110

People in Science: Erwin Chargaff, 135–136

People in Science: Francis Crick, 135–136

People in Science: James Watson, 135–136

People in Science: Lynn Margulis, 31–32

People in Science: Rosalind Franklin, 135–136

Structure of DNA, 135–136

Teaching Offspring, 191–192

TEM (transmission electron microscope), 14, 36

temperature

animals' response to, *100,* 101, *101*

effect on seed germination, 168

temporal lobe, *103*

tension, 102

tentacles, 81, 88

theory

cell theory, 13, *13*

development of, 9

Margulis's theory, 31–32

thornback ray, *142*

thornbug, 46, *46*

three-dimensional models, 25, 28, *28,* 35, *35*

thymine (T), 135

thymus, *119*

thyroid gland, *119*

tiger shark, 84, *84*

tissue, 50

of animals, 82

of heart, 51, *51*

of muscular system, 53, *53*

organization of cells into, 50

of plants, 67, *67*

skin, 51, *51*

structure and function of, 51, *51,* 53, *53*

types of, 82

titmouse bird, 123, *123*

tomato plants, 169, *169*

tools, animals' use of, 105

touch, 73, 104

toxin, 84, 131

trachea, 87

trait, 126

breeding for, 169

dominant and recessive, 127

inherited, 121, 132–133, 186

learned and acquired, 132, 139

models of, 132–134

phenotype and genotype, 130–131

selection in dog breeds, 187, *187*

study of, **126**–127

variation through sexual reproduction, 143

transmission electron microscope (TEM), 14, 36

tree frog, 178

true-breeding plant, 127

tulips, 54, *54*

turkey vulture, *102*

two-dimensional models, 25, 28, *28*

U

ultraviolet (UV) light, 102

unicellular organism, *1,* 7, **8,** *8,* 16

asexual reproduction of, 143

cell functions, 20

cells of, 17, *17,* 21, *21*

organization of, 48, *48*

Unit Performance Task

How can dehydration be prevented? 119–120

How can doctors explain what sickle cell anemia is to affected children? 41–42

Save the Whitebark Pines! 201–202

Unit Project

Causes of Organism's Behaviors, 45

Plant Perfect, 123